catify
to satisfy

catify to satisfy

SIMPLE SOLUTIONS
FOR CREATING A
CAT-FRIENDLY HOME

JACKSON GALAXY
AND KATE BENJAMIN

JEREMY P. TARCHER/PENGUIN | AN IMPRINT OF PENGUIN RANDOM HOUSE | NEW YORK

JEREMY P. TARCHER/PENGUIN
An imprint of Penguin Random House LLC
375 Hudson Street
New York, New York 10014

Most Tarcher/Penguin books are available at special quantity discounts for bulk
purchase for sales promotions, premiums, fund-raising, and educational needs.
Special books or book excerpts also can be created to fit specific needs.
For details, write: SpecialMarkets@penguinrandomhouse.com.

ISBN 978-0-399-17699-9

Printed in the United States of America
3   5   7   9   10   8   6   4   2

BOOK DESIGN BY MEIGHAN CAVANAUGH

Frontispiece © Irene R. Boniece

To the citizens of Catification Nation—

those on four legs and those on two—

without whose imagination, inspiration, motivation,

perspiration and determination, none of this would exist.

We hope we've done you proud.

contents

acknowledgments

Jackson and Kate would like to extend their sincerest thanks to the following individuals and organizations for their help in the creation of this book. Some have been around the catified block with us before, and for some, this is their first cat rodeo—but every single one has been essential in making something with so many moving parts appear effortless:

Sara Carder and her team at Tarcher/ Penguin, including Joanna Ng and Brianna Yamashita.

Joy Tutela at David Black Agency, always our champion.

Josephine Tan, Kevin Krogstad and Jessica Hano at Tan Management for keeping the wheels on the train well-oiled and on the tracks.

Norm Aladjem and his team at LEG, including Sanaz Yamin.

Liza Anderson and her team at Anderson PR, including James Weir and Melissa Nowakowski.

Carolyn Conrad at Schreck, Rose, Dapello & Adams.

Ivo Fischer, Bethany Dick, Amanda Gawrgy, Jeff Lesh, Theresa Brown and Jenni Levine at William Morris/Endeavor.

The incredible Animal Planet team behind *My Cat From Hell*, including Marjorie Kaplan, Rick Holzman, Melinda Toporoff and Pat Dempsey.

The team at Discovery Communications, including Shannon Erb, Chris Finnegan, Matt Windsor and Karin Failla.

On the production side thank you to those at 3 Ball Entertainment who have raised and waved the flag of *My Cat From Hell* for six seasons including Adam Kaloustian, Eva Mancil, Matt Allyn and JD Roth.

Nica Scott for lending her illustration skills again.

Jeff Newton for a fresh eye, steady hand, artistic mind and a definite way with the cats.

Bridgette Chesne and Maggie Schaefer at Humane Society of Boulder Valley, the backbone behind our innagural shelter Catification profile.

Many thanks to Greg Krueger, Peter Cohen and Diane Irvine Armitage for opening their homes and hearts to us and for showing the world what can be accomplished by simply asking a family member, "What can I do to make you happy?"

SPECIAL THANKS

Jackson—

Thanks to the enduring faith and grounding power of my family.

Thanks to Minoo for loving me.

Thanks to Mooshka, Audrey, Pishi, Barry, Lily, Caroline, Vivienne, Sophie, Ernie, Eddie and Oliver just for being near me.

Thanks to Heather, Siena and Toast for patience, trust and belief. And more patience.

Thanks to the team at Spirit Essences, including Debra, Celeste, Leanne, Beth, Jeff and Mojo for the elbow grease and good vibes behind the promise.

Stephanie R., for teaching me to stay right-sized and close by.

Robert D., for reminders of the promise and the occasional long-distance lasso.

Finally, I'd like this book to honor two ladies who have seen me at my worst and stood by me as I promised better:

Mama Galaxy, for teaching me early on how to love unconditionally—and today, for showing me how to live unconditionally as well.

Velouria, for showing me what life beyond the challenge line looks like. And for sleeping on my chest for twenty years.

Kate—

Thanks again to the Hauspanther team, Linda Pelo, Star DeLuna, Sara Santiago, Gerda Lobo, Mamalat and Claude. Thanks to my parents, Barbara and Don Benjamin, for cheering me on, and to Mark Allred for his enduring support. And of course, my feline family members who continuously serve as my inspiration and test subjects: Simba, Mackenzie, Ando, Dazzler, Sherman, McKinley, Andy, Bear, Sylvia, Margot and Lilly.

introduction

We are thrilled to bring you our latest collection of ideas and inspiration for catifying your home in order to create a peaceful and pleasant environment where your cat can truly thrive.

As wonderful a process as it's been to take our ideas from our first book together, *Catification*, bend and shape them, and make them—well, generally—more awesome, we are even more excited because this book represents a collaboration in the truest sense of the word: a global dialogue where inspiration turns to perspiration turns to happy cats and back again. There has been a never-ending flow of projects coming our way from you, the citizens of Catification Nation, and we have been in the enviable position of poring through this sea of amazingness and gathering some of our favorites here for you. One thing that makes us giddy is seeing projects that were directly inspired by ideas in the first book, which you'll find throughout the chapters.

This time, keep an eye out for special sections where "Jackson talks about" important concepts behind Catification—taking you deeper into the world of thinking, living and feeling like a cat than ever before. We've also tackled some of the thornier topics plaguing cat guardians, like litter boxes and scratching. With our support, you are better equipped to face these issues head-on, without fear or preconceived notions, as we work toward successful and creative solutions.

As usual, make sure to utilize "Kate's Pro Tips" as you start planning your projects, as well as tips and tricks from cat guardians whose Catification trials, errors and ultimate successes can help get you to the feline promised land with less frustration.

Last but definitely not least, we are thrilled to add in-depth explorations into some very special catified spaces. These profiles and projects from Catification Nation introduce you to unique stories of relationships that spawn inspired works.

Included in these pages are: Peter Cohen's cat paradise in Southern California; Greg Krueger's Minnesota home, which thanks to his dedication to his craft and to his cats has become almost a monument to catified nirvana; Diane Irvine Armitage's artistic catio in San Juan Capistrano, California; and an incredible renovation of the cat adoption center at the Humane Society of Boulder Valley in Colorado.

This global explosion of Catification projects indicates one thing for sure: cats are being seen in a new light, and their happiness is taking center stage. Just do a quick search on Facebook, Instagram or Pinterest for #catification and you'll see what we mean. As people devoted to the elevation of cats in our collective consciousness, we see *Catify to Satisfy* as a celebratory tribute to the creativity and commitment of a global community. We are well on the way to making the world a better place for our beloved feline family members. And, as citizens of Catification Nation, we can all agree—if the cats are happy, so are we.

—Jackson and Kate

a note from jackson

Over twenty years ago, I became immersed in the world of cats and the animal welfare movement when I was initially hired at an animal shelter. Many cats' lives were lost back then, oftentimes due to nothing more than a lack of knowledge of their inner lives. They were "other" to us; we shelter workers, as a population devoted to animal companions, "got" the language and life of dogs, but cats, while lovable, as a whole came across as distant and uncaring compared to their canine counterparts.

It was at that point that I naively dove headfirst into all things Cat (so much so that my coworkers dubbed me "Catboy"). I immersed myself completely in their world—and on their terms—and began communicating what I learned in the process to other humans, hoping this would cultivate true empathy and a deeper human-cat connection, and translate into lives saved.

Fast-forward eighteen years, when we pub-

lished our last book, *Catification*, and I finally proclaimed that it was "a good time to be Catboy!" Why? Because from the era of the desperate measures, the sticking of fingers in the dam, the bailing out of the SS *Overpopulation* with a proverbial thimble, to the publication of *Catification*, I had been privileged to be both participant in and witness to an amazing rebirth—an appreciation of all things Cat that hasn't been seen since ancient Egypt. Suddenly, instead of rolled eyes and subconscious dismissal of these magnificent, barely domesticated animals, an investment is being made; instead of lamenting what cats *aren't*, we have begun to take back the stereotype, while simultaneously exploring terra incognita with humility. That's right, humans are asking for answers and camaraderie, not just from another species, but from the "other."

This renaissance of sorts is not exclusive to the appreciation of cats from afar; the new breed of "cat person" is not satisfied to just rack up

YouTube views of Maru jumping in and out of a box twenty-plus million times. Let's face it: the "community" we call the Internet is still decidedly anonymous. If you are feeling the heat of judgment, you can always just unplug and walk away.

But that's not how the new breed operates.

The new breed doesn't just gingerly step out of the closet marked "cat person"; they bust down the door. They *own it*. Shrugging off preconceived notions (as well as their crazy-cat-lady sweaters), the new breed is art student and high-powered attorney, truck driver and goth girl, Ozzie and Harriet and Ellen and Portia and all stops in between. The bond between us, and the message megaphoned out to the rest of the world, is: *We love our cats and we couldn't care less what you think.* That's not a renaissance—that's a *revolution*.

Heady times, indeed . . . and, yeah, a good time to be Catboy. That said, *Catification* was still a risk. Sure, we were all about taking ownership of who we were . . . but were we ready to put our money where our mouths were? The message of the book, underneath the beautiful pictures and crafty ideas, was that if you *really, really* wanted to make life just that much better for your bush and tree dwellers, you would take the leap—and allow them to leap, traverse, hunt, stalk, observe from a distance or choose life in the mix. In other words, share your home by designing for both human *and* cat. First, invest in really understanding their lives, but then take it a step further and feel what it is to live in cat skin, see through cat eyes and move moment-to-

moment with Cat Mojo. It's one thing to let your feline flag fly, but another to plant it in your living room.

And again, the new breed rose to the occasion. The day *Catification* made it onto the *New York Times* Best Sellers list was . . . well, it was pretty cool, I won't lie. I was proud of *us*. That pride was reflected in the pages of the book itself; design submissions from this burgeoning global community were featured prominently and grouped into sections called "Catification Nation."

Catify to Satisfy is, in some ways, a continuation of (and a deeper dive into) the themes we explored in *Catification*. Now that the "shock and awe" of cat/human design has worn off, we can begin to address the questions posed by our readers who want to know more about the "how" and the "why."

We also thought our readers would enjoy spending more up-close-and-personal time with the "who"—the citizens of Catification Nation. Each of the highlighted stories in this book emphasizes the concept that great design contains equal measures of the technical and the emotional. The completion of construction is also the culmination of a personal journey of human lives intertwined with the lives of cats. These projects stand as monuments to that journey, and as such, we thought their stories should hold as much weight as their accomplishments. That's why we asked photographer Jeff Newton to lend his formidable skills as a portrait artist to the book—to capture the personal triumph contained inside the letters "DIY."

As I hope you can tell by now, I'm still pretty excited about where we are and where we're headed. More than anything, I hope that you can see *Catify to Satisfy* as both a reference tool and a shot in the arm. I hope you see projects that you can make your own, that you see your story and your journey reflected in the ones that we profile; and I hope you put this book down a louder and prouder citizen of Catification Nation.

In the end, I believe that your home will be a more harmonious one (not to mention cooler looking!), and if you spread the word, you spread knowledge and empowerment—and the winners will be not just the cats in your home, but *all* cats.

With Light, Love and Mojo—
Jackson Galaxy
May 2015

catify

to satisfy

base camp:
the heart of catification

In the world of The Raw Cat, territory is key. Whether your cat is a lion or a leopard, a free-roaming feral or a cozy sit-on-your-lap feline, all cats are driven to own their territory, and Cat Mojo is all about making them feel confident that they do. As you read this book, this statement (and all of the intentions behind it) will always hold true.

EVERY DOMESTIC CAT carries an ancestral twin with them. Stripped of modern conveniences, the comfy cushions, warm shelter and scheduled meals, there is a "Raw Cat" underneath—a wild animal whose survival instincts are honed to a fine point because they are positioned right in the middle of the food chain, equal parts predator and prey. Every moment in the life of your cat is informed at the instinctual level by the Raw Cat. It is critical that when we build a life for our house cats, we don't leave their ancestral twins behind.

CAT MOJO is the essence of confidence, a state of mind which, when achieved, is manifested inside and out. Cat Mojo reflects confident ownership of territory and an instinctive feeling of having a job to do within that territory. When a cat has his or her Mojo working, he carries out daily activities of hunt, catch, kill, eat, groom, and sleep with quiet confidence. It is part of who he is and makes a significant impact on how he experiences the world. In the wild, Cat Mojo in action is the key to survival; at home, it is the secret ingredient for true happiness—it allows a not-so-domestic animal to not only survive, but *thrive*.

Another truth is that confident ownership of territory starts with that territory's center, the home within the home. That center is what we will call *base camp*. In the case of the big cats, imagine a pride of lions gathered under a single Acacia tree. That tree provides shade, a measure of defense, a place to bring their kill and a place to mark (via scratching and urine marking), letting outsiders know who owns what around here.

This is where the world of free-roaming and house cats diverge. The wild ones can stake out their claim, make it theirs and defend it. If we want to create raw Cat Mojo in our house-cat companions, we must create base camp, a place for mojo to take root and bloom.

> **BASE CAMP** is a defined area of your home that is the heart of a cat's territory. It's a place of introduction and acclimation as well as a place of safety.

For climbers on Mount Everest, base camp is where they acclimate before ascending to the summit. For them, base camp is a defined area with amenities in what is otherwise hostile territory. For a cat being introduced to a new home, setting up base camp is critical in making a smooth transition.

Setting up base camp for your cats is an essential Catification tool that will make life easier for them (and, of course, you) no matter what changes may come throughout your life together. Moving, remodeling, introducing residents to new animals, introducing a new human family member (baby, partner, housemate, etc.)—all of these transitions can be minimized and tackled with so much more ease as long as cats have base camp to return to.

Speaking of major life transitions, let's start with the biggest one—the day you bring your new cat home. Knowing how important it is for a cat (regardless of age, sex or past history) to own or at least claim co-ownership of every square inch before he can confidently call his new surroundings "home," the last thing you'd want to do is open the carrier in the middle of the living room and say, "Have at it!" That's an invitation to a state of complete overwhelm, and a new housemate who spends the first two weeks under the bed. Instead, set up base camp in a space central to the home yet confined, so your cat can figure you and the territory out at his or her own pace.

Mount Everest Base Camp
© Peter Barritt/Robert Harding World Imagery/Getty Images

> A **SIGNPOST** is an object that signifies positive territory ownership for your cat, an object that the cat has claimed through visual and scent marking. Scratchers, beds and litter boxes are all examples of signposts.

In addition to defining a geographic area as base camp, you should fill it with things that signify home. Everest climbers will bring select personal items with them to base camp—photos of loved ones or a favorite blanket—in order to make it feel like home. Likewise, base camp for your cat also needs to be filled with such signposts, objects that she can own and that give her a sense of being home.

> **SCENT SOAKERS** are items made from soft materials that will absorb a cat's scent, in effect becoming a foundational signpost. Soft beds and blankets, carpeted surfaces and even cardboard and sisal scratchers allow your cat to rub or scratch and leave his scent behind, signifying ownership.

When setting up base camp, make sure to load the area with things that will become signposts. This includes anything that is a significant resource to a cat, like a litter box, water bowl or food dish. Cat condos or trees,

beds, blankets, scratching posts and other scent soakers should be everywhere in base camp. Toys, which represent a cat's prey, are important signposts and can also be scent soakers, depending on the materials they are made from. If you don't give your cat appropriate signposts, he will make his own, and you may not be happy with his choices.

SIGNPOSTS VS. GRAFFITI

You just rented your first apartment. You saved up the first and last month's rent (and the pet deposit, naturally!), you are given the key and you walk into a completely empty space, a territorial tabula rasa. You rummage through one of your many cardboard boxes and you find the sign you made years earlier when you built a tree house. The sign is scrawled in Magic Marker: SHAWN'S HOUSE—USE SECRET KNOCK! You proudly

© Devon Christopher Adams

hang the sign in the entranceway, breathing a sigh of . . . ownership.

You are a gang member in an impoverished urban neighborhood. Nothing has ever been given to you, and earning it has been an exercise in frustration. So you join a "family." You have your own language, your own greetings, a code of honor and belonging. You define the square blocks that belong to your gang. And every building, every mailbox, every phone booth is emblazoned with your family's coat of arms. Respect and ownership in this world wasn't given and couldn't be earned—it was taken—until another gang comes to the neighborhood and, claiming ownership precisely as you did, tags its name over yours.

These examples provide us with the two extremes of territorial confidence: signposts and graffiti. At this point you should be getting a glimpse of how the establishment of base camp encourages the positive beginnings of ownership. Leaving scent on beds, in litter boxes, scratching on designated furniture and doing it in a socially significant space helps head unconfident behavior off at the pass as well as the graffiti (urine marking, scratching beds and couches) that comes with such behavior. What goes in

base camp is only the beginning, however. As with any element of Catification, the "where" is just as important as the "what."

PICKING A ROOM FOR BASE CAMP

It's important to choose an area of your home for base camp that is socially significant. Ideally it should be a place where you regularly spend time. Don't use the laundry room, the garage, the basement or the extra bathroom as base camp. Base camp should provide your cat with a blueprint of what home is; it should have your scent already in it. Your cat will always return to base camp for comfort and security, so choose a space that will remain safe and accessible in the future.

It may seem like a gimme that we are referencing your master bedroom, but it's not really that simple. The master does work as an obvious choice if you have only one cat in the home, but remember, you will be needing to separate cats for a while as you get the new adoptee used to the territory and introduce him to the resident cats. In that case, the master being base camp for the new cat is probably not the best choice since it could create territorial tension. After all, the master bedroom is the ultimate "home within the home" for humans, so it will be the most desired destination for all animals. Kicking residents out while introducing newcomers will more than likely get their relationship off on the wrong foot. All this is to say: choose significant spaces, but choose carefully.

The Importance of Scent

Don't underestimate the cooperative power of scent in creating base camp. The commingling of your scent with the cat's scent is a powerful indicator of home. The combination of your scents will create comfort, familiarity and co-ownership.

BASE CAMP AND THE CHALLENGE LINE

From the day you bring your new friend home, you have the opportunity to create a dynamic relationship based on the provision of equal measures of comfort and challenge. Yes, we want to provide him with scent soakers, commingled scents, places where confidence can take root. But we have to remember that fear and small, insignificant behavior can also begin in the same spot.

BLOCKING OFF *THE UNDERS*

Once you've decided on an area of your home for base camp, you'll need to eliminate any hard-to-reach places where a scared cat might hide. Make sure to block off *the unders*—under the bed, under the sofa, under chairs, tables or other furniture. An unconfident cat will try to disappear, but we want to use base camp as a place to build confidence, so eliminating these hiding places will help your cat to find confidence in more socially acceptable spots. Plus, you'll be spending time with your cat in base camp and you don't want her hiding away from you.

© Devon Christopher Adams

It can be challenging to completely block off the space under a bed, sofa or other area, but this is really critical for creating a space where your cat will be forced to come out into the world and interact with you as he becomes more familiar with his new surroundings. You'll also want to consider blocking off *the unders* throughout the rest of your house, not just in base camp. When you do eventually let your new cat out to explore the rest of the house, you don't want him squeezing into a new hiding place.

Every little hideaway space is different, so

there's no one-size-fits-all solution. This task calls for some creativity, especially since you want it to look good! One option is to look for furniture that is naturally blocked off—sofas and beds with platform bases work perfectly, and they can also provide you with extra storage space.

If you're handy, you might be able to build something to block off *the unders*, but how about simply using that space for storing items that will do the trick? Aki Minasian from Monterey Park, California, uses the space under her dressers and bed to store her husband's growing collection of guitar cases. It works like a charm to keep her cats from caving under the furniture.

CAVING VS. COCOONING

As it is with any facet of living with cats, there is no absolute right or wrong. We want you to create comfort and challenge within your cats' base camp, but only you can decide how much of either is too much. Take away every single "hiding spot" from an already displaced and scared cat, and—instead of fostering confidence through challenge—you could be sending her into a state of territorial shock. The key to creating comforting "hidey holes" for your cat inside base camp is understanding the difference between caves and cocoons.

Caves are places like *the unders* that we want to eliminate. They are places where cats hide out in fear. Instead, you'll want to create cocoons, which are safe, semienclosed areas that are more readily accessible, mobile and not hidden away.

CAVING is a term for cats that are hiding away out of fear. They are trying to do nothing but vanish. When a cat is caving, he is trying to disappear into a dark, enclosed space where no one can find him. Often, in a misguided sense of providing comfort, we build beds and other comfy spaces under the bed or in the closet. Unwittingly we have encouraged and rewarded fear by providing caves.

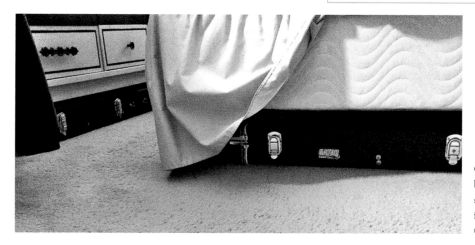

Creative solution for blocking off *the unders* submitted by Aki Minasian from Monterey Park, California.

EXAMPLES OF CAVING

CLOCKWISE FROM LEFT:

Midna, submitted by Lara Slullitel from Rosario, Argentina.

Tasha, submitted by Jillian Mills and François Beauséjour from Montréal, Quebec.

Thor, submitted by Jennifer Bull from the United Kingdom.

We can allow cats to be tucked away in secluded areas, but we need to control where these places are. A **COCOON** is such a place: a moveable hideaway you can place in socially significant areas. The cat then gets the opportunity to bring down his stress by being "invisible," and at the same time we get to bring those spots closer and closer to the rest of the world. A bed in a closet will always be just that. A cocoon can start out in the closet and slowly be moved until it is on your bed, your couch, somewhere in the center of the room—providing the unique ability to disappear in plain sight. True to their names, cocoons present us with the magic of metamorphosis, helping your cat gain confidence in his territory.

CLOCKWISE FROM TOP LEFT:

Suna, submitted by Andre from Santiago, Chile.

Fritz, submitted by Diane McLoughlin from Dublin, Ireland.

Moët, submitted by Dr. Emily Shotter from Muscat, Oman.

Bailey, submitted by Rae Wagner from Osoyoos, British Columb

Use Your Carrier as a Cocoon!

Instead of storing your cat's carrier away in the closet, take the door off (if you can) and place it in a prominent location in base camp. Put a comfy scent-soaked fabric inside it; feed favorite treats only there. Now the carrier will become a familiar cocoon and a safe place, as opposed to the association most cats have of it as a scary place, since every time it comes out of the closet, it means a trip to the vet. After your cat has established this spot as a favored cocoon, put the door back on it. That way it can easily play the role of carrier when called upon!

Moose hangs out in his carrier while at home. Submitted by K. M. Hanna from Chicago, Illinois.

QUICK AND EASY COCOON

What do cats love the most? That's right, paper bags! They make great cocoons!

Toby, submitted by Danielle Detjen from Zama, Japan.

TURF TUNNEL COCOON

Here's a fun little cocoon that you can make for your cat using materials found at any home improvement store. This cat hideaway can be placed anywhere to give your cat a cozy spot to hang out while still being part of the family. The design can be customized in a variety of ways, from changing the size to using different materials. Just follow these general guidelines and let your creativity run wild!

© Kate Benjamin

MATERIALS AND TOOLS:

- 12-in.-diameter cardboard concrete tube
- T square
- Hacksaw
- Black tape
- Awl
- 4 round wooden feet
- Screws and flat washers to attach feet
- Screwdriver
- Utility knife
- Astroturf
- Outdoor carpet
- Carpet tape (double sided)

The main structure of the cocoon is created with a cardboard concrete tube. These come in a variety of sizes from 8 inches in diameter up to 12 inches and larger. I used a 12-inch tube for this example since it gives cats plenty of room to turn around inside.

First, measure the length of tube that you're using for your cocoon. I made mine 18 inches long to allow for lounging space inside, but you could make it longer or shorter. Use a T square to measure and mark all the way around the tube; then use a hacksaw to carefully cut the tube.

Because the edges of the cardboard tube will be exposed (and it can be difficult to cut clean edges), I used black tape to trim around both ends of the tube.

Next you'll need to mark the location for the feet, before attaching the outer covering. Placement of the feet will depend on the size of the feet that you are using. I used three-inch-round wooden feet that I purchased at a craft supply store, but you could use any premade furniture foot or leg or even drawer knobs. You'll need to position the feet so that they raise the tube off the ground slightly and so they are wide enough apart to keep the tube from tipping over. You may need to experiment a little, but this is the step in which to do that. Mark the location on the outside of the tube where you will be attaching the feet and use the awl to poke a hole through the tube.

Now it's time to attach the outer covering. Measure the outer circumference of your tube and cut the material to size. I used double-sided carpet tape to attach the covering to the tube, but you many want to investigate other adhesives, depending on the type of material you're using to cover the tube. Spray glue, contact cement or construction adhesive could all work well; find one that you're comfortable working with.

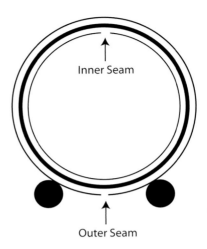

Inner Seam

Outer Seam

Carefully align the covering and wrap it around the tube, pressing firmly to adhere both surfaces together. Make sure to position the seam at the bottom of the tube between the marks for the feet. This will keep the seam out of sight and prevent cats from pulling on the edge of the covering.

In order to conceal the screws and washers used to attach the feet, you'll need to attach the feet to the outside of the tube before you attach the inner covering. I used one-inch flat washers on the inside of the tube in order to prevent the screws from pulling through the cardboard.

So Many Options!

This project can be made with a variety of different materials on the inside and the outside. Felt, carpet, sisal, even heavy fabric would all be great options. Think of all the possibilities!

The last step is to attach the inner covering. I recommend positioning the seam for the inner covering at the top of the tube so your cats won't be walking and sitting on it. Now it's time to let your cats enjoy their new cocoon!

© *Kate Benjamin*

Rusty

Our boy Rusty loves his two older cat brothers and dog sister but has always been a little skittish with myself, my husband and any human visitors. He was rescued as a kitten with his litter mates and his feral mom by a rescue group out of North Carolina. He loved to hide under things and we tried different solutions until we realized he absolutely loves burrowing into blankets. We now have blankets on furniture throughout the house and they give him a place to go for security; he sometimes even presses against my leg while under the blanket (which would never happen if he wasn't under there). He's a very special boy and we're so happy to have him as a member of our family.

—CRISTINA SCOTT, ELK GROVE, CALIFORNIA

🐾 does your cat like to cocoon in the blankets?

ABOVE: Kuro, submitted by Cissi Kristiansson from Sweden.

RIGHT: Carly, submitted by Adam Irby and Bri Monkiewicz from Sacramento, California.

ABOVE: Nero, submitted by Sydney Buiteweg from Big Rapids, Michigan.

RIGHT: Fritz, submitted by Diane McLoughlin from Dublin, Ireland.

Hank and Dean, submitted by Jane Ann Wynn from Parkville, Maryland.

CREATIVE COCOONS

Patrick and Kate Pacacha from Williamsport, Pennsylvania, created a cozy cocoon for their cats by removing the bottom drawer in their dresser. Of course, the drawer was immediately claimed as a bed!

Tigger Chewbacca and Bongo Bongo, submitted by Patrick and Kate Pacacha from Williamsport, Pennsylvania.

Kethry

Kethry is a very nervous cat. She always seems to feel the other cats are hunting her. I have given her several areas in the house where she can feel like she's part of the family but safe, too. This was my solution in our breakfast room. It serves the additional purpose of giving my husband a place to put his work bag where the cats won't play with it or scratch it.

—KERRI SHER, PITTSBURGH, PENNSYLVANIA

MOVING BEYOND BASE CAMP

Once base camp has served its initial purpose of providing your cat with a strong sense of territory ownership—or, in other words, that feeling of "I'm home"—then it's time to start introducing her to the rest of the house. All of those signposts that have been helping to define her territory in base camp will become tools (a yellow brick road of ownership, you might say) that serve to expand your cat's territory in a way that continues to build her confidence and keeps her feeling at ease.

> **BASE CAMP EXPANSION** happens when you move signposts from base camp out into other parts of the house as a way to introduce your cat to the rest of your home.

When your cat is ready to start exploring beyond base camp, pick some key signposts—maybe a litter box, a scratcher or a well-used bed—and place them in the hallway or in the next room. Now when your cat ventures out, she will encounter these objects that already have her scent on them, helping her feel like this must be home, too.

It's important to keep in mind that for an object to truly become a significant signpost, it has to actually be used by the cat in base camp. If there's a scratching post in base camp that never gets used, it won't become a signpost just by osmosis. Be aware of which objects your cat really owns through use when they are in base camp.

Base camp expansion has another side, also—call it *base camp rotation*. Every time you remove something from base camp and move it to another location in your home, replace it with something new to "marinate" in the familiar surroundings of base camp. This way you'll always have a new crop of signposts that can be used to create territorial security throughout the house. Don't worry about replicating the original piece; just use the knowledge you've gained about favored materials, placement in the space relative to doors, windows, and human furniture and allow it to marinate with base camp mojo. Then, as you catify throughout the years, these signposts, big and small, can ensure continued comfort and easier adaptation through life's challenges.

Finally, base camp expansion and rotation are incredibly useful tools in a multicat household; as marinated signposts are scattered throughout the home, other cats get to meet the newcomer in a decidedly less confrontational manner, and they can, in turn, put their scent on it to establish co-ownership of the territory.

How Long Should I Keep My Cat in Base Camp?

There's no simple answer to this question because every cat is different. Some cats will arrive in a new home and almost immediately feel at ease, holding their tails up high, showing that they're ready to be a part of things. Others may take longer, acting skittish at first, even, as we've already discussed, trying to hide or become invisible. You may discover that you have an "overowner," a cat that's marking everything as a way to gain confidence. In any case, the most important thing is for you to observe your cat and really pay attention to what he or she is telling you through body language and behavior. Be patient and attentive and you'll know when it's time to move beyond base camp.

ONGOING USES OF BASE CAMP

Just as climbers on Mount Everest return to their base camp after taking excursions, cats will return to base camp. It becomes their place of security, a place they can always return to and feel at home.

Base camp will be especially helpful in situations that are potentially stressful for your cat.

Perhaps you are having guests over; make sure that base camp is accessible and well stocked with food, water and clean litter so your cat can spend the party in her comfort zone. The same would go for renovations in your home, another situation that might cause your cat to retreat to her safe space.

Base Camp as Ground Zero in an Emergency

In the event of an emergency in which you might have to evacuate with your cat, having a clearly defined base camp can serve you well. If your cat knows that this area is the default place to go when something is unusual, it could make it much easier to round him up if you need to corral him and get out. This example provides us with an even stronger argument for blocking off *the unders*. The last thing you want is your cat, in the midst of an emergency, winding up under the dresser or so far under the middle of the bed that you can't easily wrangle her and evacuate. I'm not being an overprotective cat daddy here; I have unfortunately known cats who have died in fires when they put themselves in the smallest possible space within their home to escape a house fire. So we are beyond just blocking *the unders*. Do a thorough sweep of your base camp room and think of any place where your cat could squeeze in. When in doubt about it being too small, don't underestimate her abilities to disappear and play it safe. No hiding place should be left untouched and unblocked.

Another aforementioned concept also comes in handy: turning her carrier into a destination, a place of safety. Having your cat actually *choose* to head for her carrier in dire times makes your job of evacuating safely just a little bit easier. Think about what makes a hiding place a destination and try to replicate it. For instance draping a blanket over the carrier and putting it in a corner will go a long way toward providing a safe space that works for both you and your cat. Also, multiple cats call for multiple "evacuation pods." You literally can't overdo it when trying to point your cats toward a workable emergency rendezvous spot.

Please see "Blocking Off *The Unders*" for more information.

As we alluded at the beginning of this chapter, you will find base camp very useful when introducing someone new to your household. For instance, say you're planning to bring in a new roommate, or possibly a significant other is moving in. Try placing something with the person's scent on it (a towel or a sweater, for example) in base camp in order to introduce them to your cat. Think of it as a virtual handshake using scent. You don't want your new roommate to arrive and have all of her belongings marked by an unconfident, overwhelmed cat.

The same goes for introducing a new baby to your cat. Use the comfort of base camp as the place to make the virtual introduction by bringing in baby's scent. Follow this with the reverse and place some signposts from base camp in the baby's nursery so when your cat visits the baby's room, she feels at home there, too.

And, of course, bringing home a new dog or cat can be stressful for resident cats, so make sure to use base camp as a tool for both current family members as well as new. Introducing them on either side of the door to base camp, giving them equal but separate access to the room, is an ideal way to slowly introduce them.

No matter what your commitment is to catifying your home, either financial or aesthetic, base camp works. After all, your cat needs belongings just like you do—that shouldn't be a luxury. This way, all of her favorite stuff is part of a plan to keep her confident no matter where you call home or who you share that home with. Base camp is not just a destination; it's an indispensable part of the journey as well.

faces in the nation

Diane Irvine Armitage,
San Juan Capistrano, California

Diane merged her passion for art with her love of cats to create an incredible kitty wonderland.

"WHEN THE STUDENT IS READY, THE TEACHER WILL APPEAR."

—*traditional Buddhist proverb*

© *Jeff Newton*

As the story goes with so many citizens of Catification Nation that we've encountered, Diane grew up with cats, but never felt she was a "cat person" until the right cat showed up at the right time and changed everything.

What makes Diane's journey just that much more serendipitous is the fact that she also grew up surrounded by art. Her father is a professional artist and illustrator, and she grew up immersed in that world, following in his footsteps, even working, as a teenager, in her parents' art gallery and frame shop, where she would sometimes sell her watercolors. She later worked as a graphic artist and experimented with decorative arts, including stained glass and mosaic work. But just as with cats, art was a part of her life, not an obsession—until the student was ready.

Today, Diane and her husband Dave (a cat lover himself) have built what she calls "my own little world," where her passions live and thrive; every nook and cranny reflects a love for and dedication to cats and art. And the thing that becomes obvious, as one explores this "little world,"

is that it reflects in design the emotional transformative journey they've been on together.

Diane and David first adopted a senior cat named Buster. David formed a bond with Buster, who lived to be sixteen. But even after Buster's passing, Diane still didn't consider herself "a cat person." Next came a stray kitten they named Pandora, or, as she's more commonly called today, "PD." But, Diane explains, that still didn't change the way she saw herself: "Even when PD showed up and was a supercute little fuzzy kitten, I still wasn't that into cats. Somewhere around when PD was about one year old, I just suddenly got the cat bug."

Diane started to realize how well cats complemented her own personality and lifestyle. "I just kind of get them; I feel comfortable with them," she says. "I think I really like cats because of

their independence and how quiet they are. I tend to be a loner and like quiet pursuits, like reading and art, and cats are perfect companions for someone like me."

Once Diane started to open up to the idea of being a student to the cat/teacher, her true education began in earnest. "I learned a lot from my cats about letting go of trying to control someone. You really can't control cats! You can encourage them to do something different, but they have a mind of their own," Diane reflects. "I found that instead of trying so hard to get them to do things my way, if I turned it around and saw things from their perspective, then I could help them to have what they wanted (instead of forcing what I wanted). And when I learned to relax and let the cats do their thing, life became much nicer and it actually became fun to see what the crazy cats would do next. I began to empathize with the cats and tried to see things their way, and that's what led to our Catification projects."

ASK NOT WHAT YOUR CAT CAN DO FOR YOU—ASK WHAT YOU CAN DO FOR YOUR CAT

All of a sudden, Diane truly understood the concept of looking at the world through the eyes of a cat. She also started to observe how differently people look at cats. "Some people ask, 'What can you do for me? Are you going to snuggle with me? Are you going to be my companion?' while I look at it like, 'What can I do to make your life wonderful?' Just being around the cats is good enough for me."

ART AND CATS

While Diane's understanding and connection to cats was flourishing, she was also exploring her interest in oil painting. When laid off from her job a couple of years ago, she joined a "painting a day" community of artists, who paint something small every day to develop their skills. Soon, she found herself completely hooked on oil painting, and in a beautiful convergence of her two new passions, decided to paint only cats, especially black ones. "I painted them small, I painted them huge—I used a lot of black paint."

She continued to explore oil painting, learning about different styles, until she found one that spoke to her. Now she creates beautiful portraits of cats on colorful backgrounds, capturing their personalities with sketchy brushstrokes.

Dare we say that Diane's newfound love of cats ignited her latest artistic endeavor? The proof is in the painting. All one has to do is look into her subjects' eyes; there is an emotional presence there which reflects an artist who understands deeply what lies behind those eyes, and who is equally passionate about relaying that life to the viewer. Diane's portraits represent empathy in art, and that comes only when the artist surrenders to her subject. It will come as no surprise that these works of art were to become prominent features in Diane's Catification showcase: her new outdoor catios.

EXPANDING THE TERRITORY

Around the same time that Diane was starting her oil paintings, she and David decided to tackle their first Catification project. "I saw the cats trapped in a tiny house looking outside— they really wanted to be outside—and I felt that. I wanted to make it happen for them." Diane needed to find a way to give them access to the outside but still keep them safe.

Phase 1—Covered Catio

Dane and David's catio project happened in phases. The first phase involved enclosing an area under the stairs outside the building that Diane uses as her studio, which is separate from the main house. A cat door leads from the studio out to the catio that was enclosed with metal mesh. Inside the enclosed area Diane added a large cat tree and heated beds for chilly mornings. This part of the project took about a month to complete, and the cats loved it immediately.

Window — Tunnel PHASE 3

ART STUDIO

MAIN HOUSE

Open Catio PHASE 2

Window Above
Cat Door Below

Covered Catio PHASE 1

Cat Door

Cat Door

Phase 2—Open Catio

The novelty of the small catio area eventually wore off and Diane noticed the cats looking out toward the strip of grass on the other side of the wire mesh wall. A year after completing phase one, Diane and David enclosed a much larger area of the yard at the back of the studio, expanding the cats' territory further. The new area is open on top, so they used polycarbonate panels and cat fencing to keep all the cats inside. This special fencing is set at an inward angle to prevent cats from climbing up and out, and it works like a charm. The large open catio connects to the original covered catio with a cat door in the wire mesh wall between the two areas, allowing Diane to give the cats access only to the smaller covered area when she wishes.

© Jeff Newton

Angled fencing and polycarbonate panels prevent cats from escaping.

Diane grows lots of cat-safe herbs and grass in the large open catio. "They love it when the grass is nice and tall because they can act like big cats in the wild, stalking their prey through the tall grass." There's also a big, shallow bowl for drinking water hidden amongst the tall grass so the cats can pretend that they have stumbled upon a small pond when they are looking for a drink.

© Jeff Newton

Potted plants and play tunnels provide plenty of spots for cats to lurk, waiting as if in the wild, ready to catch their prey. Human seating makes the catio an attractive and inviting area for the whole family. And of course, Diane created giant portraits of her cats to adorn the walls of the catio. "The cats don't care at all about the décor, but I do," says Diane.

© Jeff Newton

Phase 3—Tunnel

And finally, just this year, Diane and David added the finishing touch to this amazing project. They built an enclosed tunnel connecting the main house to the studio, allowing the cats full access from the front of the property all the way to the back. Now the cats have a racetrack, which Diane reports is used several times a day by a couple of her girls traveling at lightning speed.

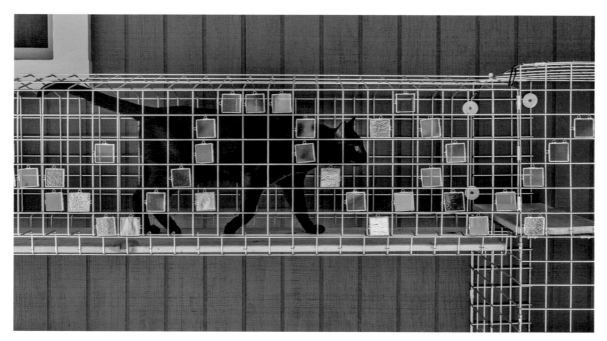

They purchased a premade system of wire mesh tunnels that can be completely customized to accommodate almost any home. The tunnel starts at the main house, where the cats can access it through a cat door. It runs along the back of the house and up a few steps, then across to the studio building, back down a few steps and in through the front window. The window can be closed off to prevent access into the studio.

Window from tunnel into studio

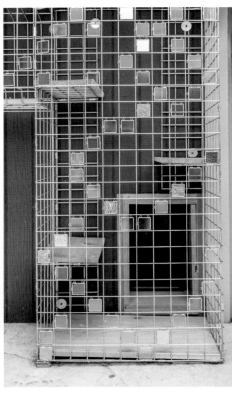

Cat door from tunnel into main house

© Jeff Newton

The tunnel gave Diane a blank canvas where she could add an artistic touch: "As an artist, I found the oversized chicken coop-look of the tunnel a bit hard to take, so I started brainstorming to try to find ways to make it more visually fun. I was inspired by an art installation that used iridescent glass in the holes of a chain-link fence, so I thought I might try something similar on the tunnel. I cut 2-inch by 2-inch squares of dichroic glass (dichroic glass changes colors depending on the angle at which you view it and also with the changing light—sort of like a dragonfly's wings), then I soldered the squares like one would do for a stained glass window, then attached them with small rings to the tunnel. I used a minimum of rings because I wanted them to move slightly with the wind. The light catches them and sends dancing fireflies onto the bricks below in the afternoon—it is really magical."

SITE-SWAPPING

Diane's catio design is impressive, but the way she uses it with her cats may be even more so. Diane uses a concept Jackson calls site-swapping. This is when only certain cats have access to specific areas at designated times. This is a system born from necessity; Diane currently has five cats and a mix of challenging personalities— which means not everyone gets along.

Morticia (black) and Luna (tuxedo) are the best of friends and they stay together constantly. Mille is not a fan of other cats, but she mostly keeps to herself and doesn't cause any problems. Bela is the newest member of the household and is still getting oriented after recovering from some health issues.

© Jeff Newton

And then there's Pandora. She showed up in Diane and David's driveway as a tiny stray kitten, meowing and covered in fleas. They took her in and tried to introduce her to the other cats, but her aggressive behavior has proven too risky for unregulated commingling, so Diane strategically uses the catio and tunnel to manage everyone and maintain the peace.

Because Diane built in several ways to close off different parts of the catio and tunnel, it works perfectly for site-swapping. Pandora is allowed access to certain parts of the catio and buildings at specific times of day and the others (who all get along) are in another area. Then they can switch when needed and everyone stays out of harm's way.

The Same Rules Apply

We asked Diane what advice she would give to someone who wanted to start creating art, and the answers she gave were quite interesting because you could easily substitute "catifying" for "creating art":

"You just have to start." Exactly! Don't let the idea of creating/catifying stop you dead in your tracks; just pick a project and go for it!

"It's all just practice." Again, applies to both: the more creating/catifying you do, the better you will get.

"There are a whole bunch of rules that you kind of follow, and then you can break them later." This concept is absolutely integral to our overall approach and message: we're giving you some rules in this book. Know them well, internalize the concepts so you are in the best position possible to get the job done. Then, and only then, it's up to you to go and learn the rest from your cats—and break those rules as needed.

"Once you learn the rules, you'll look at things differently; you're going to see things that you never saw before because you weren't looking for it." Put on your cat glasses and you'll be amazed at what you see!

Start Simple

Diane's three-phase catio project might seem a bit ambitious, but don't let it overwhelm you when applying it to your Catification vision. Her advice is to start small, with something like Cat TV (see page 204 for more information on Cat TV). This is a great project that's easy for anyone to do. It's the best way to watch cats be cats and it has an immediate payoff.

Before Diane even thought about building the first catio, she started with Cat TV herself. "I built a little area in my bedroom where we

put a bird feeder outside the window. There's a tree incredibly close to the house, so I hung the bird feeder in it. There was a little shelf by the window that the cats used. They'd just sit on the shelf looking at the bird feeder. Now there's a bookcase there with giant pillows on top. It's like being in a cat lounge up there! They watch the birds all day. They are glued to it. It's a great project to start with and it's easy to expand from there. I built out from the top of the bookcase, adding a big shelf and carpeted climbing tubes."

Don't Get Hung Up on Aesthetics

Finally, Diane reminds us that Catification can be pleasing for everyone. "You know what I find is the biggest stumbling block? It's people who are so into the aesthetic of things. That's what stops a lot of people from catifying. They just don't want to change the look of their home in a way that they consider to be less aesthetically pleasing." Diane has shown us that art and function can come together to create something that everyone will love, and reminds us that "Catification isn't just for cats, you know."

© Jeff Newton

Billy, submitted by Lisanne Bouwman from
Venray, the Netherlands.

2

scratching solutions

If there is one simple visual that represents the ultimate territorial tug-of-war between humans and their feline companions, it's the sight of claw marks. Whether fraying the fabric of a favorite piece of furniture, or whittling vertical streaks in a doorjamb or horizontal racing stripes on your carpeted stairs, you can rest assured that the two species see two very different things: the human sees an aggravating eyesore, while the cat sees a welcome signpost.

There really is only one way to head this potentially divisive stare-down off at the pass and, in turn, make everyone happy. As the title of this book suggests, you can indeed catify to satisfy. And, as always, it begins with *you* understanding *them*.

KNOW YOUR CLIENT

Our starting point in this case is the behavior of scratching and, more specifically, how it applies to the larger picture of your home. We want to first step out of the role of dedicated family member and into the shoes of interior designer. Our job is to "know our client," and the best way is from the outside in. Start with the needs of ALL cats (Cat with a capital "C"), the givens of behavior based on evolution, biology and historical adaptation, and drill down until we explore the specific needs of *your cat*—what makes him unique, his individual character quirks, possible physical limitations and what he or she likes or needs to do (to our amusement and/or chagrin). The following are key concepts toward the end of knowing "Cat."

THE MARK OF OWNERSHIP

You have a collection of photos in beautiful frames displayed on your mantle. They are carefully arranged by date and importance of the relationship. You dust those pictures, continually readjust them by mere inches to better catch the light, sometimes reorder them because you just so happen to be reminiscing about a certain time and place. These mementos are not just there so that you can remember those good times whenever you walk by; on a certain level, they also give you a sense of territorial security—a moment when, either consciously or subconsciously, you remind yourself, "This is *my* home and this is *my* life." In other words, you gain confidence when given proof of ownership.

The pictures and the mantle provide for you what something as simple as a scratching post can provide for cats. Walking by, they catch their own scent soaked into the fabric, and briefly regard their visual mark as well. As you would, at that moment, adjust a framed picture, they reach up and give the post a vigorous dig and pull, making that satisfying scratching sound, releasing scent from the scent glands and getting a sense of security and ownership. That scratching post has now, in the world of Cat, transformed from mere furniture to essential signpost.

WHAT'S MINE IS YOURS

In a perfect world, cats would stick to creating signposts out of scratching posts. However, we're sure you've noticed that your cat *really loves* to scratch on the sofa, or your bed or your favorite chair. The main reason these work so perfectly for cats is precisely why they don't work for us—they are key territorial destinations. (The couch seems to be a favored scratch target more than any other place. See the sidebar for more reasons why.) More often than not, when we come home, we settle into these comfy destinations, and over time they become human scent soakers. Just add up the amount of time you spend, per day, between your bed and the couch. Probably close to nine or ten hours? Your cat just wants to commingle "marks," making these places superior signposts since they reflect the ultimate bond of family through co-ownership.

JACKSON TALKS ABOUT . . .

Why Does My Cat Scratch on the Sofa?

There are a few key ingredients that, when put together, become the perfect storm for scratching, better known as your sofa. Since your cat wants to complement your scent with hers, and since we tend to spend so much of our free time on the sofa, it is a veritable gold mine of potential ownership. In addition, the sofa is usually covered in a wonderfully scratchable material—if it feels nice when you sit on it, you can be certain that it feels just as nice between your cat's claws. Then there is the sturdy construction: cats are not just leaving marks, but are also exercising the upper part of their bodies and trying to remove dead nail sheaths. Unfortunately there aren't many scratching posts around that can take that kind of pulling and dragging without tipping over. The arm of the sofa will never, ever tip. Keep these things in mind when choosing scratchers for your cat—you may never be able to replicate the exact ingredients of the perfect storm in one magical piece of furniture, but now you know what ingredients you're looking for and, as we know, that's power for solving cat issues and keeping them solved.

SCRATCHING AND *YOUR* CAT

Location, material and angle preference give you insight into not just your cat's personality, but also what will work for him as you try to find a more acceptable scratching surface. In the sections that follow, we will look into the world of *your* cat as opposed to *every* cat.

Location. As we've been discussing, a cat's scratch mark is a pretty universal declaration of territorial ownership. However, underneath the surface of just about any such generality lies the preference of the individual. In other words, every cat will seek to put a mark on what he or she perceives to be socially significant; your cat will tell you what areas he considers significant in part by how many times he returns to the spot to scratch it. One of your cats might pick the sofa, while another frequents the rug in the hallway. Just as we've found previously in the sofa example, these areas are usually just as important to us as they are to them.

For example, let's say that your cat is scratching on the doorjamb outside your bedroom. What's he telling you? First and foremost, he's telling you that the bedroom is pretty significant to him. Smart cat! For the vast majority of us, the bedroom is the seat of the entire territory. So, in essence, he's putting his name on a welcome mat in front of the bedroom—the symbol of family and at the same time a warning to those perceived as outsiders that this area is important . . . and is definitely not theirs.

Of course, while location is an integral piece of the scratching puzzle, it is still just that—a piece, two other important pieces still remain . . .

Materials. Observing what your cat scratches around your home is an opportunity for you to choose wisely when it comes to the texture of scratchers that you provide as an acceptable alternative. Cat scratchers can be made from cardboard, carpet, sisal, cork, wood, etc.

Ideally the scratching surface lets your cat dig in his claws and rake them through the material. Cats may have a preference for certain materials and may even dislike others. You'll need to figure out which material your cat likes best in order to encourage maximum scratchability.

 scratching materials

COMMON MATERIALS FOR CAT SCRATCHERS:

Cardboard	Carpet	Sisal Rope
Sisal Rug	Wood	Cork

© Kate Benjamin

Angle. Next, look at the angle at which your cat likes to scratch, based on what she has marked up around your home. Does she scratch carpet or your stereo speakers? Gentle vertical inclines like stairs, or more severe verticality like the arm of your couch? Your cat may be sending you messages that she prefers a horizontal surface, or maybe a scratching area that's at an incline. Of course, these preferences are somewhat

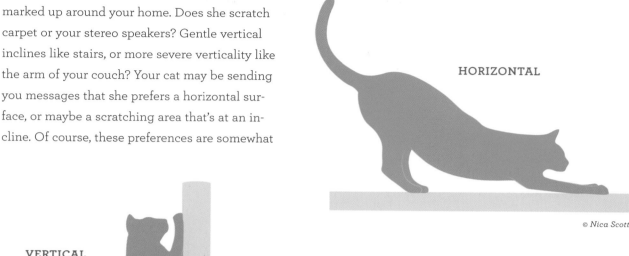

🐾 scratching angle

HORIZONTAL

© Nica Scott

VERTICAL

INCLINE

fluid throughout a cat's life, but tapping in to your observational skills can help minimize the chances that you will spend a good deal of money on a cat scratcher that *your* cat will never, ever use.

With the preceding three factors in mind, let's revisit the example of your cat having a penchant for scratching the doorjamb outside your bedroom. Now we have even more information about who he is in relationship to scratching. Now we know that he considers the bedroom an essential social area, plus he's a cat who likes the texture of wood and prefers to scratch vertically.

What about your cat? Completing the following worksheet will give you all the information you need to make informed decisions about finding solutions to the behavior that work for both human AND cat.

WORKSHEET

WHAT?

What material does your cat scratch on?

- ☐ Cardboard
- ☐ Carpet
- ☐ Sisal rope
- ☐ Sisal rug
- ☐ Wood
- ☐ Other ______________________________

HOW?

How does your cat like to scratch?

- ☐ Horizontally
- ☐ Vertically
- ☐ At an incline

If your cat scratches vertically, does he or she scratch down low by the floor or up higher?

- ☐ Low
- ☐ High

WHERE?

Where in your home is your cat scratching?

- ☐ Living room
- ☐ Dining room
- ☐ Bedroom
- ☐ Office
- ☐ Kitchen
- ☐ Other ______________________________

How much time do you spend each day in these areas of your home?

- ☐ Living room ______________________________
- ☐ Dining room ______________________________
- ☐ Bedroom ______________________________
- ☐ Office ______________________________
- ☐ Kitchen ______________________________
- ☐ Other ______________________________

Totoro

Everyday life with my kitty Totoro has been very easy and problem free! He is just an awesome and wonderful kitty! There is one exception . . . scratching posts! Yep, when Totoro started to find out how to use his claws, we tried three different kinds and he rejected them all! I mean he avoided them like the plague, and one of them—he would walk around it as if it had some sort of barrier! That was until we got him a scratching mat that he loves and uses every day, I guess because it's easy for him to use. We only spent $11 on the scratching mat—that's it!

—CHAZZ R., TUSTIN, CALIFORNIA

© *Kate Benjamin*

PUTTING IT ALL TOGETHER

Now that you know your client, you can really begin to work for her, so that your interest are not at odds with each other. It's time to catify to satisfy the need to scratch, and in the following section we give you techniques and hints so that you can take your newfound tools and turn them into methods.

My Cat Won't Use the Scratcher I Bought for Him. What's the Problem?

First, you have to ask yourself the tough question: Did you buy that scratcher (a) because you read this chapter, learned about your "client," filled out the worksheet and then shopped appropriately? Or (b) because you liked it (or it was on sale, or it was the first one you found)? Don't forget, Catification is all about compromise, so if your cat won't scratch, there's a good chance you prioritized your own tastes over what you know to be your cat's needs.

If you followed all the dos and don'ts outlined here and your cat still won't use the new scratcher, here are two extra hints: First, have patience. One of the reasons we are having you test things is that you have to see what sticks. And in order to give it a chance to stick, you have to give it time.

Along with patience, take a closer look at the location. Being in a strong territorial spot is crucial, but allow yourself to compromise between a spot of ownership and one of pleasure—that is to say, putting the scratcher near a window may not be effective from a territorial or tactical standpoint, but supplying a sun-drenched crow's nest where the day can be spent binge-watching Cat TV (traffic, human and animal neighbors, etc.) is blissful. And, at the end of the day, happiness is just as much an ingredient in our Mojo recipe as ownership.

NO/YES FOR SCRATCHING

The "No/Yes" is a cornerstone concept when it comes to training an animal (or human, for that matter); it also speaks to the very heart of achieving a successful relationship with your cat (or anyone else). How do you get what you want while at the same time getting the cat to think that he too is getting what he wants? The thing to remember is that behind every "No!" there also has to be a "Yes!"

Let's begin with the "No!" by making the inappropriate scratching surface unappealing—a "nondestination" for your cat. One effective way is to cover the surface with something that a cat will find offensive or unpleasant to the touch, such as double-sided tape. This will very simply achieve our ultimate goal immediately since he can't sink his claws in without feeling the "Ewwww!" Aluminum foil, the underside of an office chair mat or rubbery shelf liners can also be unattractive to cats and can be used to cover surfaces temporarily until your cat has started using the acceptable scratching surface regularly.

Cat-Deterring Materials

Double-sided tape

Aluminum foil

© Kate Benjamin

Office chair mat (upside down)

Shelf liner

Look for special tape at the pet supply store that's designed specifically for deterring cats from scratching while not harming your sofa.

Heavy-duty office chair mats are another useful tool when creating the "No." You'll need heavy shears to cut the mat, but the little spikes on the bottom will be unpleasant for cats to walk on.

Cats don't like the feel of aluminum foil or rubbery shelf liner, both of which are easily found and inexpensive. Experiment with these materials until you find something that does the trick!

Now, before you start panicking about living with a sofa covered in tape, breathe . . . and remember this: we are in the process of *training*, not *designing*. Once we have forged a new relationship between the cat and his chosen target, we can ditch the tape!

Now that we have the "Ewwwww!" in place, it's crucial to have the "Ahhhhh!" ready to go. First and foremost, use the tools we've been discussing to find the best scratcher for the job based on location, texture and angle.

If the goal is co-ownership of the couch—an area that's important to both you and your cat—the scratcher needs to be perceived as *part of the couch.*

In terms of angle, your cat has told you that she prefers vertical scratching if she is using the entire side of the couch. In addition, she's also told you a little more about the quality of the angle itself (see sidebar on page 43).

When it comes to material, well, it goes without saying that she likes the texture of your couch. It makes it that much easier to find a complementary texture for your "Yes."

Sturdy and Stable

It's important to choose a scratcher that's stable so it won't topple over and scare kitty when she tries to use it. The last thing you want is for your cat to be afraid of the new scratcher you bought for her and to never use it!

The idea here is to make the "Yes" a means of *immediate gratification.* In the moment of impulse, there is an appealing and rewarding alternative that offers a multitude of benefits that the "No" does not. As the "training" continues, long-term gratification takes over—your cat recognizes her mark and experiences that crucial jolt of territorial ownership.

Saku
© *Lanz Chester Enterina*

When I got Saku, he was the sweetest, most energetic little kit I've ever known. He was quickly potty trained and we had zero problems with him in our little condo. But years later, when we moved to our big house, he felt the need to mark everything by scratching all of my dad's precious furniture! My dad got so mad that he warned me that either Saku had to learn not to scratch anything expensive or he had to go.

I tried to think of alternatives to catify the house without ruining my dad's dream interior. I learned that cats don't like sticky things, so for a few days I placed some double-sided adhesive tape on the areas where Saku would scratch—the sofa headrest, the armrest and behind the sofa. Then I placed substitute fancy cardboard boxes behind the sofa to redirect his attention. And since Saku's old scratching posts didn't interest him anymore, I bought him a bigger scratching post that also serves as a playhouse for him. Catification was very effective, and Saku no longer damages the furniture, so I get to keep him forever.

—KATS DEL ROSARIO, PARAÑAQUE CITY, PHILIPPINES

How Many Scratchers Do I Need to Have in My House?

There's no real formula for the number of scratchers to have, but we recommend erring on the side of one too many. Basically, if you're still having problems, add another one.

The Bad News and the Good News Is the Same News

A "bad news" discovery doesn't have to end in frustration and dismay. Inherent in every single piece of bad news is an opportunity. If you have four scratchers in the living room and your cat has just picked a fifth spot to scratch, ignoring all of your attempts at providing the "Yes," see it as a way to learn more about your client. Instead of screaming "WHY ME?" ask "Why?" Detaching from the emotion of the moment and being a cat detective will always have payoffs—the least of which is having fewer gray hairs!

WALL-MOUNTED SCRATCHERS

Wall-mounted scratchers, or scratchers that you actually attach to the wall, are great for small spaces because they don't take up any floor space, but they are also great because you can hang them at any height. This is the best way to accommodate cats that like to stretch up nice and tall when they scratch as well as cats that prefer lower vertical scratching closer to the ground. The other advantage to wall-mounted scratchers is that, when properly installed, most styles are extremely sturdy. If the scratcher is mounted securely to the wall, there's no chance of it falling over and startling kitty!

© Kate Benjamin

Wainscoting Scratching Wall

Submitted by Teri Trujillo, Riverbank, California

Teri was searching for a wall-mounted scratcher but didn't like the look of any she found for sale, so she decided come up with her own design. Instead of making small, individual scratchers, Teri made an entire scratching wall that actually looks like wainscoting.

MATERIALS:

- 1×3-in., 1×4-in. and 1×6-in. boards
- Sisal carpet
- Spray adhesive
- Decorative wall trim
- Paint and stain

Teri cut the sisal carpet into 11-inch by 30-inch pieces and then used the spray adhesive to glue the sisal directly to the wall. She painted and stained the boards and used them to trim around the sisal, nailing the 6-inch board to the bottom, the 3-inch boards between the sisal pieces and the 4-inch board across the top. She added the decorative trim (also painted and stained to match) to cover all the edges of the sisal. This is a great idea because it prevents cats from pulling at the edge of the sisal and unraveling it.

The end result is a completely integrated Catification element that matches Teri's décor and is extremely functional for her cats. "It's attractive and my cats LOVE to use it," Teri reports. Even after two years of use, the scratching wall is still looking great. Bravo, Teri!

REPURPOSED PICTURE FRAME WALL SCRATCHER

I was inspired by Teri's awesome wainscoting scratching wall, but I was thinking that some people might not want to tackle such a large project, and they might not want to glue the sisal directly to the wall. Instead, why not find an old picture frame and make a decorative wall scratcher that you can hang anywhere?

MATERIALS AND TOOLS:

- Old picture frame, no glass
- Sisal rug remnant (can also use carpet)
- Heavy paperboard
- Spray adhesive
- Scissors
- Straightedge
- Utility knife
- Heavy-duty tape
- Wall anchors
- Screws and finish washers
- Screwdriver

First, I found an old picture in a frame without glass at the thrift store for only $6. I carefully removed the picture and then cut a piece of heavy paperboard to the same size as the opening in the back of the frame.

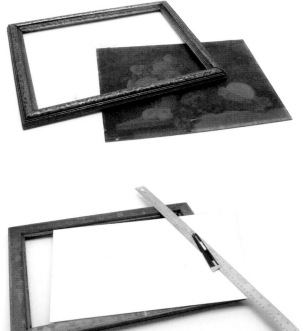

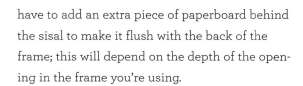

Next, I cut the sisal rug remnant to the same size as the paperboard and glued the sisal to the board with the spray adhesive. I secured the sisal and board inside the frame with some heavy-duty tape around all the edges. Note: you may have to add an extra piece of paperboard behind the sisal to make it flush with the back of the frame; this will depend on the depth of the opening in the frame you're using.

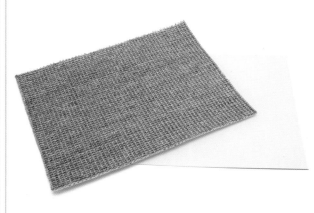

© Kate Benjamin

The edges of the sisal should be hidden behind the frame to prevent fraying.

I used four screws with finish washers and wall anchors to secure the scratcher to the wall. I chose a location down low and near the front door where the cats spend a lot of time (it's also right outside the kitchen!). As you can see, it's a big hit!

© Kate Benjamin

When Should I Replace My Cat's Scratcher?

It's probably time to replace your cat's scratcher when the surface has become completely worn out, to the point of being so smooth that it's no longer useful. However, you might want to hold on to that old scratcher because it's now a great signpost that could be a useful tool for helping your cat claim her territory.

FOUND OBJECTS AS SCRATCHERS

When looking for things for your cat to scratch on, think outside the box a little. You don't have to purchase just regular old cat scratchers—you can be creative! Thrift stores have all kinds of fabulous finds that can easily be converted into cat scratching heaven, plus they won't break the bank.

An old ottoman or footstool could make a great cat scratcher.

© Kate Benjamin

DIY PROJECT

THRIFT-STORE-FIND CAT SCRATCHER

I ventured out to the thrift store to find something cheap and unique to make into a cat scratcher. Hidden at the back of the store was a small decorative wall shelf for $5. When you're on the lookout for unusual items to catify, sometimes you have to turn things on their heads (or in this case, on its side). This little shelf caught my eye because it was good looking and sturdy, and it had the right measurements for a cat scratcher; plus, the price was right!

© Kate Benjamin

MATERIALS AND TOOLS:

- Thrift-store-find shelf
- Board for base
- Paint
- Screws to attach base to shelf
- Screwdriver
- Sisal rope
- Glue gun and glue sticks
- Nonslip feet

This project may be done slightly differently depending on what kind of treasure you find in the thrift store. With this particular shelf, I needed to attach it to a larger base in order to make the scratcher freestanding and sturdy enough for cats to use without tipping it over.

The shelf measures 24 inches tall when placed on its side, so I cut a piece of ¾-inch-thick plywood into a 20-inch square to use as the base. If you have the tools and the skills, you can rout the edges and round the corners. I painted the base black to match the shelf and added nonslip stick-on feet to the bottom in order to prevent it from sliding on hard floors.

To make the scratching surfaces, I wrapped ⅜-inch sisal rope around both sides of the shelf, securing the rope with hot glue as I wrapped it around.

The next step was to attach the scratcher to the base. In this case I predrilled the holes and countersunk the screws in the bottom so they wouldn't protrude and scratch the floor.

ADD A CAT TOY!

In order to add a little incentive for the cats to check out the scratcher and to make it more of an entertainment center, I created a simple hanging cat toy to dangle from the top in between the two sides.

MATERIALS AND TOOLS:

- Ping-Pong ball
- Rice
- ⅛-in. shock cord
- Scissors
- Awl
- Lighter

© Kate Benjamin

Make an easy dangling cat toy to add to your thrift store creation! It takes just a few simple materials. Use an awl to poke a hole directly through both sides of a Ping-Pong ball. Drop five to ten grains of rice inside the ball to give the toy a gentle rattle. Thread ⅛-inch shock cord through both holes and tie a knot at the bottom. Leave enough cord on top to attach the toy to your project and allow it to hang where kitty can bat at it.

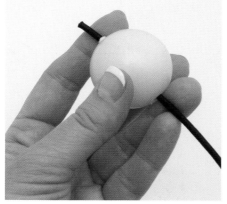

Kate's Pro Tip

Melt the ends of the shock cord with a lighter to prevent fraying. This will also make it easier to thread the cord through the Ping-Pong ball.

Sylvia is lured over by the dangling toy.

Andy gives the scratcher a try.

© Kate Benjamin

Ando decides that it makes a
great perch, too!.

NATURAL SCRATCHING SURFACES

Outdoors, cats will naturally scratch on trees and logs, so why not bring a little nature inside for kitty to sharpen her claws on? A piece of an old tree limb can make a beautiful and functional scratcher for no money at all. (Note: whenever bringing a piece of natural wood inside to make a scratcher or other climbing structure, make sure to check it for bugs first.)

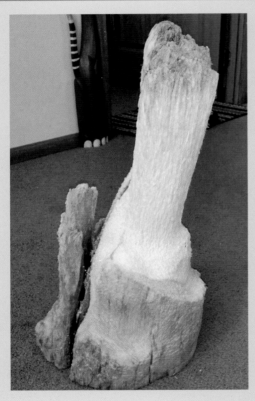

© Jodi Summers

This log has been used by cats in our family for more than thirty years! They love it.

—JODI SUMMERS, AUSTIN, COLORADO

THERE'S NO PERFECT SOLUTION

The nature of cat scratchers is that they shred and leave bits of material scattered on the floor. It's just part of the deal. Some materials will shred more than others, but, just as with cleaning the litter box (which we'll get to next!), don't let the scratching shreds get you down. Try to make it easy on yourself and store a broom and dustpan nearby so it's a breeze for you to sweep up on a regular basis. You don't want to be tracking shreds all over the house. Consider getting a small cordless vacuum and placing it strategically by your cat's scratcher so you can just grab it and take care of the shreds. Make it part of your regular routine!

Kate's Pro Tip

Carpet Tiles for Scratching

I'm a huge fan of carpet tiles for all kinds of Catification projects, especially for creating scratching surfaces. What makes carpet tiles so functional is that they have a sturdy backing that helps prevent the carpet from fraying on the edges, plus the backing keeps the carpet nice and flat, making it very easy to use carpet tiles in craft projects.

Carpet tiles come in a huge variety of colors and textures. The carpet fibers, called pile, can be

© Kate Benjamin

looped or cut. Cats may prefer cut pile over looped because the cut pile will allow them to rake their claws through the fibers, whereas their claws can get caught in looped pile.

Cut pile

Looped pile

ALTERNATIVE SCRATCHING MATERIALS

You don't have to stick with traditional scratching materials; be creative and find something different that will work for your cat.

Consider using a yoga mat to create a DIY cat scratching surface. Yoga mats let cats dig their claws in, plus they are cheap and easy to find and come in a variety of colors. They are really simple to cut with just a pair of scissors. Plus, if you recycle your old yoga mat for kitty, it will already have your scent on it!

I found these cork tiles in the office supply section of a store. They are meant to be used as bulletin boards, but you can easily attach them to the wall and let kitty use them as a scratching surface.

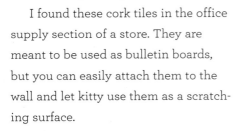

© Kate Benjamin

Kate's Scratchtastic Scratching Center

Here's a peek at the scratching center in my living room. We have horizontal, vertical and incline scratching surfaces plus carpet, sisal, cardboard and wood to choose from. That's pretty much something for everyone!

Peter Cohen
Goleta, California

As the co-owner of a custom building firm in Southern California, Peter Cohen had no limits when creating a paradise for his cats—and his compassion for all cats is equally unbounded.

In 1995, when Peter Cohen first started catifying his home in Goleta, California, he never imagined that twenty years later he'd still be adding catwalks and passageways—and more cats.

It all started when he bought the house in 1988 and it came with two outdoor cats. Peter, who had until that point lived only with dogs and had even been allergic to cats as a child, started caring for the cats. He then lost one of the cats to a car accident, and not long after the other was severely injured by a car. As he nursed her through extensive surgeries to repair her leg, he was struck by how completely dependent on him she was—and, similarly, how dependent all cats are on humans. To keep her safe, he made her an indoor cat, and to keep her company, Peter adopted two kittens from the shelter. And a "cat guy" was born.

Over the years, Peter and his housemates added more kittens to their family a couple at a time. As part of a remodel in the 1990s, they started to design and build catwalks and other Catification features to keep their growing feline family active and entertained.

Peter enlisted the help of carpenters from his building firm, Trillium Enterprises, to help with the construction. When they built the first catwalk, Peter was afraid that the cats might not use it, but they proved his fear unfounded by jumping on to the walkway even before it was complete.

© Jeff Newton

COMPASSION FOR CATS AND ALL ANIMALS

As Peter continued to work on the project, his understanding of and compassion for cats grew. "Cats provide unconditional love," Peter says. "I can provide for these cats and they return

© Jeff Newton

it ten times over. There's nothing like coming home after a stressful day and relaxing with a purring cat on your lap."

For Peter, animals are family. He recently moved his father into a nursing home that accepts and encourages pets, so his father is able to keep his beloved dog with him. "They realize that the dog is part of his family, and not some kind of property that can be thrown away."

NOT THE "CRAZY CAT GUY"

Over the years, Peter has found himself fighting the "Crazy Cat Guy" stereotype. He even named one of his cats Secret, because he didn't want to tell anyone he got another cat. "When we had as few as six, I remember my family saying that we were insane."

© Jeff Newton

ADOPT! ADOPT! ADOPT!

All of Peter's cats are adopted from shelters or rescues. He admits that the hardest part is going to the shelter and trying to decide which cats to choose. "We try to pick cats that are hard to adopt—bent tails, black cats, behavior issues, etc." Peter knows he can't take them all home (although he would like to!), but by adopting and working with rescue groups he's doing his part to help.

PLENTY OF SPACE TO OWN

With 2,400 square feet to work with, Peter has plenty of space for all of his cats, even when the numbers reach close to twenty. However, if not properly Catified, even that much space could become a war zone with so many cats. Because he has added superhighways, cocoons, scratching posts, litter boxes, Cat TV (see chapter 4) and other features throughout the house, the cats aren't fighting over the same territory. Peter notes that he never sees more than two or three cats at a time; they don't seem to congregate all in one area. Also, when the cats aren't getting along, they all find their own spaces to chill out, and peace is restored.

HOW TO DESIGN WITH CATS IN MIND

Peter really understands the importance of knowing your client when it comes to Catification. He says, "When designing for cats, I'd encourage people to put some effort into understanding what the cats want, what makes them happy. One of the problems is that we look at animals through human eyes. It's important to realize that what an animal needs isn't always exactly what a human needs." In other words, Put on your cat glasses!

BASE CAMP IN ACTION

Peter uses the base camp concept quite successfully. He designed the house so that all of the tunnels can be locked and certain parts of the home can be blocked off. If a cat is acting out, he simply puts the cat in an isolated area, which becomes a safe place, the cat's own base camp. He finds that even when he opens the area back up to the rest of the house, the cat will stay in the base camp room or retreat there in times of stress.

© Kenji Fukudome

PETER'S TIPS FOR DESIGNING YOUR CAT SUPERHIGHWAY

"Catwalks are like living sculpture," Peter explains. They are built to be visually appealing to humans and enticing for cats. There's no better way to incorporate cats into your décor than to provide them with a beautiful, functional cat superhighway. With so much experience building catwalks and superhighways, Peter provides us with some of his tips:

© Kenji Fukudome

No Dead Ends

What's the number one rule of the cat superhighway? No dead ends, a rule that Peter is intimately familiar with. "We always build catwalks with multiple exits. The cats don't like dead ends; they don't like to be trapped," Peter points out. "Early on, we made some mistakes and built catwalks with dead ends, and the cats quickly learned not to go there. Until we fixed it, they didn't use it."

Avoid Choke Points

We were introduced to a new term when talking to Peter about his cat superhighway. He describes narrow lanes where two cats can't pass each other as "choke points." If one cat is able to sit in a lane and stop the others from passing, this is a choke point.

"We always make sure that the walkway cannot be blocked by one cat," Peter explains. "We try to include an alternate route that's easy and obvious." When two cats meet each other on a narrow walkway, either they are going to fight or one's going to back down; if they have multiple ways to go, that makes it much easier. It's important to anticipate where the choke points could be and give the cats alternate ways around.

We asked Peter how he and his design team avoid creating choke points. "We think of the cat walking on the walkway, and then we imagine another cat blocking the path. Then we ask ourselves what will happen," he explains. "If they have a place to jump left, right, up or down, even if they don't use it, they feel safe. If the only option is for them to back up, then they won't feel safe."

areas of the house where the catwalks are a bit higher—twelve to thirteen feet—Peter has added wooden dowels to enclose the catwalks. These areas are still open visually, but the dowels deter cats from making dangerous jumps off the high catwalks.

© Mauel Flores

Safety First

For safety purposes, most of the catwalks are at standard ceiling height, about eight feet, but in

Peter has also tried to avoid building catwalks in areas where the cats might jump down onto humans (bed, sofa, etc.). No raining cats in the middle of the night!

The house is filled with signposts that the cats can own. Scratchers and cocoons are strategically placed along the superhighway as destinations and rest stops so cats can feel right at home everywhere they go.

Water features, including an indoor koi pond, provide the cats with plenty of stimulating Cat TV. Peter reports that no fish have ever been harmed by a cat!

© Holly Lepere

With this many cats, of course, litter boxes are everywhere, but you'd never know it. They are all concealed in closets with built-in ventilation systems, and there are some in the garage, too. The cats can access the litter boxes through tunnels that always have multiple entrances so no one can guard the litter area and create an ambush zone.

© Kenji Fukudome

Another very important design consideration that Peter paid careful attention to is making sure that every inch of the walkways and tunnels can be easily reached by people for cleaning purposes and in case of an emergency. He never wants to have a cat out of reach.

© Holly Lepere

As with every Catification project, Peter's house is a work in progress; he is constantly adding features and testing new ideas. The cats are always willing to give their feedback on whether or not they like something, but it sounds as if Peter has a pretty good understanding of who his clients are.

© Jeff Newton

The Story of Cookie

Cookie—Peter's favorite cat (Shhhh! Don't tell the others!)—was traumatized as a kitten and would attack every human who came near her when she was first adopted. It took Peter three months to get her to trust him, but now she sleeps by his side every night. "When cats suddenly start trusting humans again, the feeling is amazing," Peter tells us. Because the catwalks allow her multiple avenues of escape, she feels safe and doesn't need to run away. "She's always more confident where she can escape."

We asked Peter, "What do you get out of building things for your cats? What's in it for you?" He replied, "There's no bigger reward than the unconditional love you will get from helping a cat live a better life," Peter says. "I created a beautiful life for them in this little bubble; it just feels great to look at my happy pack."

EXTENDING CATIFICATION TO SHELTER DESIGN

When asked how he would approach redesigning an animal shelter that has a cold feeling, Peter says that he believes that the "plan," the aesthetic, is not something that just springs to life

from a blueprint. In his mind, as reflected in the look and feel of his home, compassion is the birthplace of design: "It's not really a money thing," he says. "It's how you look at animals. You can look at them as cattle or you can look at them as sentient beings. I think any time humans look at animals as sentient beings, the result will be way better."

As Peter continues to think about shelter design, he reflects on the shelter he has provided for so many cats, and on his unexpected second life as a cat lover, builder and animal advocate: "I think there's a big change coming, when people think more deeply of animals, and laws are starting to reflect that, too. Cats are not property. They are animals entrusted to our care, and if you have that view, then you would build a shelter accordingly."

© Jeff Newton

3

let's talk about
litter boxes

t's time to address the elephant in the room—what every cat guardian attempts to avoid like a trip to the dentist. That's right, the litter box. We know you hate it, but the fact is that litter boxes are one of the most, if not *the* most, significant places in your cat's territory, both from a functional standpoint and as a social signpost.

What makes the litter box such a source of contention—and often the cause of epic Catification stalemates—isn't your cat's needs, but yours.

---

t wasn't long after I started my private practice that I went to the home of a woman who had a pretty significant litter box issue. Judy had over ten cats, but more than enough room to accommodate them all. One entire side of her living room was glass—it was one of the largest windows I'd ever seen. There were off-white drapes that ran the length of the window, and the entire curtain was stained—from floor to about a foot up—yellow with pee.

Judy was absolutely beside herself—she'd had the drapes cleaned numerous times and even replaced once. She said the cost was astronomical, and her nerves couldn't take it anymore.

Looking at the situation from a behavioral standpoint, I felt that the resident cats perceived a significant threat—perhaps feral cats had taken up residence in Judy's yard. Her cats had a natural reaction, setting up a boundary between "them and us." My solution seemed obvious enough: we would work on identifying the feral population, fixing them and making sure they weren't being fed near her windows. BUT until that issue could be fully addressed, we would start by putting three litter boxes against that window, spread out evenly to territorially cover the space safely, giving her cats the signposts that they clearly were demanding.

When I explained my plan of action to Judy, she wrinkled her nose, folded her arms and began pacing in front of the window, slowly shaking her head and muttering. Finally she turned to me.

"I don't think so, Jackson," she replied as though she were somewhat insulted. "You have to understand, I LOVE my cats. I spend so much of my life, and SO much money on them. . . ."

I could feel the "but . . ." hanging in the air.

She continued, "But I have worked my entire life to afford this home. This room?" She gestured widely to underscore her point. "And that view? That's what sealed the deal for me. I knew this was the house for me. . . ."

When I tried to respond, she waved me off.

"I just won't do it, Jackson. I have to draw the line somewhere."

"But here's the thing—I just told you that if we put these three litter boxes out against this wall, then this problem could, and should, decrease significantly."

"I know, Jackson. I just have always told myself that I would sacrifice so much for my cats. But my living room is that one place I just don't want a litter box, let alone three."

"But Judy . . . look at this place. Your living room *is* a litter box."

The long and short of it was that I left without the satisfaction of having solved a pretty horrific problem, and my client replaced her drapes again, choosing to allow history to repeat itself. Most important, I had come face-to-face, for the first time, with "Litter Box Resentment."

Cats aren't the only fiercely territorial species in the home. We *tolerate* the idea of living side-by-side with our cats' waste, but introduce the idea of moving litter boxes into the open, removing the lids, and allowing them to be more available to the cat? Then, suddenly, we are at *that place*—where cats' biological and social needs come squarely up against human domestic desires and aesthetic sensibilities. When those two forces collide, we have Litter Box Resentment."

While it's not fair to assume that *every* cat guardian has experienced litter box resentment, it is fair to say that *most* of us have. Once we admit that there is a box-shaped challenge line between us and our cats, we can go about the job of litter box Catification. Only when we learn to see things from our cats' point-of-view can compromise take place. In other words, it's okay to hate the litter box—we feel you! It's just not okay to let that hate dictate every decision you make.

As we move through the next section, we'll help you figure out the number of litter boxes you need, where to place them in your home, and whether they should be covered or uncovered. Wherever you fall on the litter box resentment spectrum, it's okay—there's no judgment to be had here. We just present ideas and solutions that allow you to cross your challenge line with a measure of ease, confidence . . . and, dare we say, style!

Now . . . let's dig a little deeper!

> "It's okay to hate the litter box, but it's not okay to let that dictate every decision you make."

To Bury or Not to Bury

Cats have a natural instinct to bury their waste in order to avoid attracting predators. They will instinctively look for soft, loose material that's easy to dig into. This hardwired behavior makes it relatively easy to litter train a kitten. On the other hand, dominant cats may leave their waste exposed as a way of marking their territory. Yet others, especially "bottle babies"—cats who were fostered and brought up by humans and not their own moms and siblings—develop idiosyncratic habits like not burying simply because there was no "monkey see" for them to "monkey do"! Although the wiring is the same in all cats, the expression varies wildly.

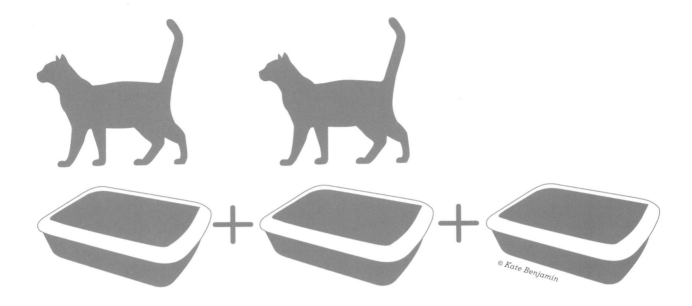

© Kate Benjamin

THE PLUS ONE RULE

How many litter boxes do you need in your home? There's an unaccredited rule of thumb that says: count your cats and then add one. So, if you have two cats, you'll want three litter boxes.

Why does the formula exist? Most would say off the bat that it's because cats don't like to share, so by having this many, everyone can claim one for himself or herself. There may be truth in that, but that's not the most important

reason, in our opinion. As we've said, it's more about the fact that the litter box is a crucial signpost. And as you know by now, one can never have enough reminders that he or she is "home." With multiple cats, it's a wise move to encourage territorial dialogue within the group, and in the absence of a spoken language, pee and poop work just fine. That said, this formula works as a general guideline. Do your cats count? No, but they will be sure to tell you if there aren't enough boxes in enough places.

The Plus-One Shortcut

I can't even begin to count how many times I've toured a home, noticed a dearth of litter boxes, and explained the "plus one" guideline. I also can't count how many times I've gone back to the home and seen the "Plus One Shortcut" executed, as if it's a collective avoidance technique.

What I'm talking about is when someone unveils three litter boxes side by side in the basement or garage.

As I did in each one of these homes, I'll have to burst your bubble as well, if that was your plan. Think for a moment about the doormats in and around your home. You probably have one at each door—front door, back door, garden door, etc. If you place them all at the front door, it doesn't accomplish much. Each one serves to mark a different area of your home and define your territory. Each mat serves as a signpost. Likewise, litter boxes define territory, and when you place them next to each other, you're defining only one area. Three together count as one. You might as well just use one large litter box. At the end of the day, it's not about the numbers, but what they symbolize.

LOCATION IS EVERYTHING

As with scratching surfaces, litter boxes are one of the most socially significant places in the home for your cat. They are the ultimate scent soakers! There's no other area of the territory where your cat's scent is stronger, so the litter box is an important signpost that really signifies home.

That leads us to the next "Catification gut check." It logically follows that litter boxes are best kept in areas that are socially significant for cats. These areas will unveil themselves to you as you observe your cats day to day, establishing themselves in certain areas by scratching, resting, stashing toys (or treats) and practicing prey techniques. In other words, areas of ritualized activities are the most socially significant.

It's also a given that wherever the human scent is the strongest, the cats will crave a sense of co-ownership.

Yes, we're walking down that road: What are the most important human/cat meeting grounds? Where is your scent is the strongest? Where do you spend the bulk of your time when home? In most cases that would be the couch and the bed—the living room and the bedroom. Think about where your cats tend to scratch the most. Probably the sides of the couch and the box spring of your bed, leaving both visual and scent markers.

Less confident cats may also spend a great deal of time by the windows and doors, especially if you have neighborhood cats outside. If your cats are spraying in these areas, they are communicating with a megaphone, saying to anyone outside, "This is mine!" Avoid the megaphone (and the graffiti) by putting a litter box by those windows or doors.

JUST CHECKING IN!

Now, before you throw this book down and walk away from the negotiating table, take a breath and remember the first requirement of Catification diplomacy: the willingness to compromise for the benefit of the greater good. Here are some important points that may prevent you from making a hasty exit:

1. Catification can (and should) be seen as a series of experiments rather than a series of permanent, life-altering choices. Remember the mantra "Try it before you catify it." Move your challenge line; put some signposts in socially significant areas and see how it feels to live with it for a week. How do the cats change the way they relate to one another and to the space in general? Notice how okay or not okay you feel about it—and then decide.

2. If there's just no way you're going to put a litter box in your living room, then please make sure you have plenty of other signposts. You can't erase all proof that cats live in your house. Recognize that you're subtracting from your cat's confidence in his or her territory by not putting a litter box in certain places, so you'll have to make up for it with other territory markers. The same goes for the bedroom, or wherever you spend the most time.

3. We are here for you! We hope that the ideas and projects that we present here will allow you to make litter boxes less intrusive for you, while still being attractive to your cats and retaining their signpost significance.

TYPES OF LITTER BOXES

There are several types of litter boxes to choose from and countless styles within each category. You'll need to find one that works for both you and your cat.

OPEN LITTER BOXES

This is a basic litter pan and is usually the least expensive option. Most are rectangular but there are also designer styles that are round or oval. Some have high sides, which are helpful for cats that stand when they pee or for cats that kick litter outside the box. Open litter boxes come in all sizes, from very small (for kittens or for traveling) to extra large. Most open litter pans are made of plastic so they are easy to clean. Some are designed specifically to fit in corners. You can also find disposable litter pans made from paper pulp or cardboard.

COVERED LITTER BOXES

Also called hooded litter boxes, these boxes are enclosed, usually with a removable dome or cover. The cat usually enters through a door, which can be on the side of the box or on the top (these are called top-entry litter boxes and are helpful for keeping dogs and children out of the box. Get more tips for keeping treat-seeking dogs

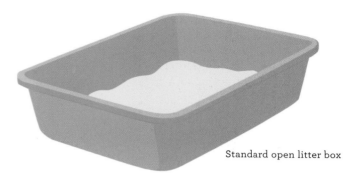

Standard open litter box

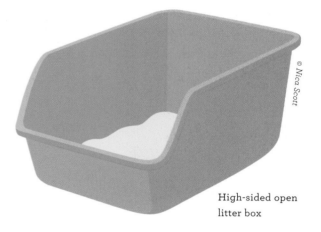

© Nica Scott

High-sided open litter box

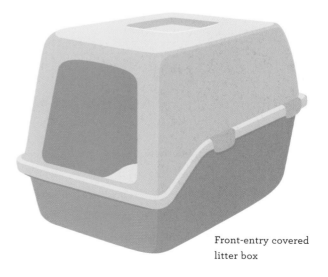

Front-entry covered litter box

out of the litter on page 110). Covered litter boxes are meant to conceal the litter box and to control odors as well as litter tracking outside the box.

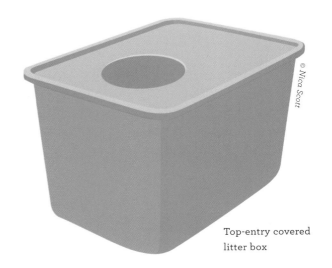

Top-entry covered litter box

AUTOMATIC SELF-CLEANING LITTER BOXES

There are several models of self-cleaning litter boxes that automatically remove solids using a raking system or other method. These are generally quite expensive and come in both open and covered styles.

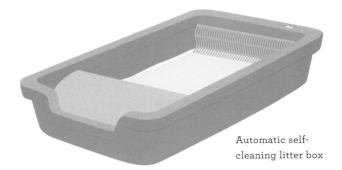

Automatic self-cleaning litter box

JACKSON TALKS ABOUT . . .

Automatic Self-Cleaning Litter Boxes

I don't like them. There. I said it.

I don't like them because, like it or not, monitoring your cat's waste is a crucial part of parenting. Think about it; if you are walking your dog, you are by default observing every time they "go potty." You even pick up their poop and discard it. During that process you get uber-important info. You may observe blood in her urine, diarrhea, evidence of worms, straining to go or frequent attempts, which leave spots of urine instead of a stream. For the next few days you will most likely step up your vigilance in watching what they eat and their general behavior, and perhaps you'll wind up calling the vet.

So when you have zero evidence and therefore zero information about your cat's waste, you have a massive gap in knowledge about his general health. Remember, cats are remarkably stoic about pain, programmed to hide weakness from predators. They will not give you demonstrative signs of discomfort. Rather, you have to find those signs. And with these types of litter boxes, those signs are, literally and figuratively, flushed away.

On a more personal, pet peeve level—I don't like them because they are just a symbol of lazy guardianship. I get it; nobody likes seeing, let alone handling, waste. But you gotta do it. Take that ridiculous sum of money and invest it in cat furniture or more toys. Spend a few minutes a day and *scoop the box*. It is a job that, pardon the pun, goes with the territory.

Choosing the Right Size Litter Box

Generally speaking, the litter box should be about one and a half times the length of your cat. When in doubt, go bigger.

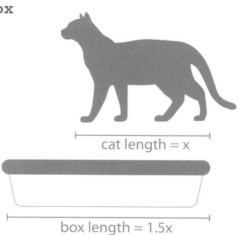

cat length = x

box length = 1.5x

HOW TO CHOOSE?

Before investing in one type of box, remember to "try it before you catify it." Litter boxes are not expensive, so try several different types and let your cats tell you what they prefer. You have to know your client, and you may need to negotiate with him or her. That's acting in the true spirit of Catification. In other words, ask yourself why you are choosing a specific type of litter box: Is it because you like the look of it? Is it because it matches your décor? Was it on sale? We're not saying that these factors are irrelevant, but don't make that color, or shape, or price point *the* deciding factor, or your cats may ignore it. And then, hello litter box resentment!

There are some pointers, depending on who your cat client is.

THE ELEVATOR-BUTT CAT

This is the cat who may start by squatting when he pees, but then, it's "elevator going UP!" and soon enough he is standing upright and soaking everything around the box. Obviously, a high-sided litter box is the best answer to this problem. It's pretty much impossible to train a cat away from this behavior; most of the time, it's something they took on very early in their lives, during the critical period of social development. It's much easier to build a better mousetrap . . . or, in this case, a pee trap. Look for a high-sided litter box that has the cut away for entry/exit on the long side; this way your elevator-butt cat

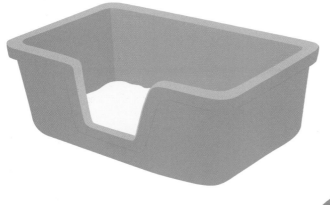

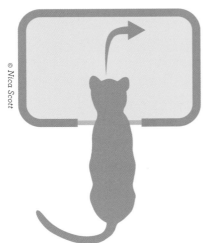

© Nica Scott

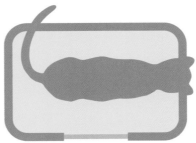

A high-sided litter box with entry on a long side encourages cat to turn when entering the box, preventing accidental peeing out the entrance.

won't simply walk into the box and pee out the door, because upon entering the box, she will be facing the shorter side and will be more likely to turn so her butt is not facing out the door.

LONG-HAIRED CATS

One thing you may notice is that if your cat has long hair, he will often not want deep litter in his box; when the litter touches the hair on the back of his legs/butt area, it tends to create a sensation that he's not comfortable with. Perhaps it's a ticklish feeling—but in any case, having about ¾-inch of litter in a long-haired cat's box seems to work wonders.

OBESE CATS

Low-sided boxes are best for obese cats. Remember, if they are having trouble getting into the box, they will eventually start thinking *that place* is just too much trouble, abandon ship and begin peeing nearby where it didn't take a herculean effort to get in. Remember also the rule of thumb about the size of the box: bigger cat means bigger box. Finally, if your "big-boned" cat has to remotely squeeze through the opening of a hooded box . . . he won't.

SENIOR CATS

The same recommendations that we give for obese cats go for seniors as well. Arthritis is a common culprit when your senior cat begins to avoid the box. With creaky hips/knees/paws, a high-sided box will look decidedly unfriendly— and that chunk of carpet under the pool table? Now that's the ticket! Also watch litter level in the box—when the litter is too high (for example, four-plus inches high), and your senior cat squats to go (especially to poop, when he has to hover over the spot), often he will start to sink into the litter, causing a grabbing motion with his toes to keep balance in the mountain of litter. Again, think primarily of arthritis in this case—if his toes already hurt, this could be that one thing that would lead him to abandon the box.

COMBO CATS

You may have a cat who is a special combination of these cats. Take, for instance, long-haired, overweight senior cats. One specific tip for them is to watch out for the covered box. Why? A long-haired obese cat trying to get through the plastic opening often winds up getting a small but perceptible static shock. If you were that cat, and you were given the choice between covered and uncovered, which would you choose? Exactly!

Make Your Own High-Sided Litter Box

Submitted by Stefanie Beyeler, Thun, Switzerland

Stefanie has an elevator-butt cat, so she made her own high-sided litter box by cutting an opening in the side of a plastic storage bin. Notice how she made the entrance on the long side so her cat would walk into the box and turn sideways before peeing. Stefanie reports that it works like a charm!

© Stefanie Beyeler, Katzentipps

LITTER BOX ISSUES

Eliminate the Ambush Zones

One thing we've seen time and time again in multicat or dog-cat homes, or even homes with young children, is a cat in a litter box getting ambushed either during elimination or upon exiting the box. Of course, that's the last thing you want to happen since it will cause your cat to avoid a decidedly unfriendly place. Negative associations with the litter box can cause ongoing issues, specifically, finding new spots that they consider safe, or at least more friendly.

You'll want to place the box in an area with a view of all angles. This means you should avoid placing the box in a closed-off area with walls on three sides; instead, allow space around the litter box so your cat can see if someone else is approaching.

Maximize the Sightlines

If your covered litter box is in a corner, angle the opening out from the corner, giving your cat the widest possible view from the entrance. Cats should be able to see most of the room. When you put a hood on a litter box you're directing the cat's path for entering and exiting. Create as much of a visual spectrum as you can.

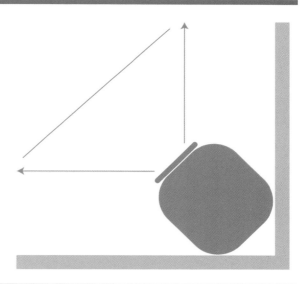

Now that kitty can see what's going on around her, make sure to provide multiple escape routes. If another cat or a dog does approach while your cat is in the box, she shouldn't be trapped with only one way to get in or out. Pretend you're standing in the litter box (we know, just humor us) and another cat is walking up to the box. What are your options? How many different directions can you go to exit the box? Only out the front entrance? Over the side? Maybe up to a low shelf or table above? Make sure there are at least two clear exit routes.

Out of Sight, Out of Mind

Covered litter boxes, as well as litter boxes that are hidden far away in remote parts of your home, may not get scooped regularly. This is a big issue! As much as you may want to hide that litter box away, you could be doing yourself a disservice.

Good placement for your cats is good placement for you, too. We're asking you to put litter boxes in locations throughout your home where your cat can easily access them. Your cat is walking through the house and, "Hey, look! There's a litter box. I think I'll use it instead of peeing on something else."

Same for you. You're walking through the house and, "Hey, look! The litter box needs scooping. I'll just take care of that now." Bam! It's that easy! No excuses, no out-of-sight-out-of-mind. Everyone will be happier, trust us.

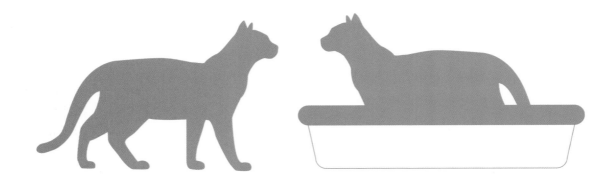

DIY PROJECT

MAKE A SIMPLE DECORATIVE LITTER SCREEN

Before you think about enclosing the litter box entirely, consider using a decorative privacy screen to shield the litter box from sight. This allows you to leave an ample amount of room around the litter box and eliminate ambush zones, depending on how you position the screen. We recommend positioning the screen to allow for entrance/exit from both sides of the box. Also, leave some space between the box and the screen so kitty can navigate all the way around the outside of the box without bumping into the screen.

© Kate Benjamin

MATERIALS:

- 2 24-in. × 36-in. corrugated plastic sheets
- Straightedge
- Utility knife
- Heavy-duty tape
- Decorative wall decals

This is an easy project that can be completely customized to match your décor. I used sheets of corrugated plastic, but you can use regular old cardboard or foam board. The advantage to using the plastic corrugated material is that it can be easily wiped clean with a damp cloth.

I used a utility knife to score both boards as shown in the diagram. Scoring means cutting through just one side of the board so you can fold the board along the cut; but do not cut all the way through. This creates a hinge so each board can be folded as shown.

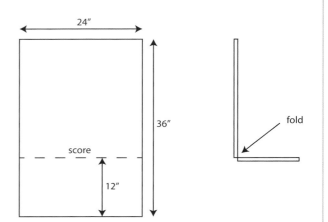

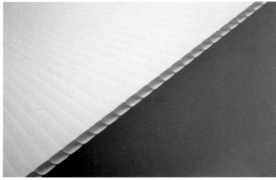

Next use the heavy-duty tape (I used white tape so it would disappear) to attach both boards together above the score. Make sure to tape on the opposite side from the score mark. This creates another hinge so the boards can be folded toward each other, forming an angle.

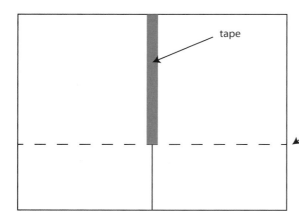

Now for the fun part! Decorate the front of your screen (the side without the tape) however you like. I used wall decals, but you can also use contact paper or, if you're artistic, pull out your paint and markers and create some original art.

To use your litter screen, fold both boards at the score marks and then make an angle with the taped hinge. You can adjust the angle to fit your needs. Place your litter box on the two over-lapping pieces on the floor. The weight of the

litter box will prevent the screen from tipping over.

I added a self-adhesive hook on the back of the screen for hanging the litter scoop, plus there's room behind the screen for a small trash can for scooping.

How convenient!

© Kate Benjamin

This project can be fully customized to suit your style and your space. Not only can you change the decoration on the front, but you can also adjust the height and width of the boards. Just make sure that the boards extend under the litter box for stability. You can even make a screen with three panels to surround the litter box a bit more.

Recognize that this project is a compromise. We're asking you to put a litter box in the living room, but you'd rather hide it. Maybe give this a try instead.

© Kate Benjamin

If you're not that crafty, you could always purchase a decorative screen to place in front of your litter box, like this one used by Shelley Kitzrow from Lake Tomahawk, Wisconsin. Screens like this come in every size and style. There are even small screens (only a few feet tall) that are perfect for adding some litter box privacy.

© Shelley L. Kitzrow

Harry's Custom Litter Crate

Submitted by Pilar Gómez, Zaragoza, Spain

Pilar decided to keep her cat's litter box right out in the open (bravo, Pilar!)—in the corner of the dining room, no less. Instead of just leaving the standard plastic box showing, she created this adorable wooden crate for her cat Harry. She painted it white and lined it with cat comics so Harry has something to read when he's in his bathroom.

This just goes to show that you don't have to enclose the box entirely to disguise it or add it to the décor. The creative possibilities are endless!

© Pilar Gómez

Harry

MAKING IT WORK
FOR EVERYONE

Which brings us to the next point: in addition to picking the right locations, as we discuss on page 100, in your home for your litter boxes, you also have to make the organization of each litter box area work for everyone involved. Think about it. There really are two litter box users: your cat and you. Your cat uses the box for her business but you are responsible for cleaning it. That means the area needs to function for both of you.

And by "function" for you we mean it has to be easy to access for cleaning purposes, because, again, if the litter box isn't being scooped regularly, you're asking for problems.

First, make sure your litter box is in a location that you can easily reach for scooping and cleaning. You'll also need to be able to sweep or vacuum regularly around the box to pick up scattered litter. Make it easy on yourself and keep this in mind when choosing a location for your litter box. You'll probably find that if an area is easily accessible for you, it's also a good choice for your cat.

Organization around the litter box is going to be different for everyone and every situation, but generally you are going to need the following items:

- Litter scoop
- Trash bags for collecting waste
- Something to hold the trash bag while scooping, like a small trash bin (this is optional but can make it easier)

- Broom and dustpan for sweeping up scattered litter
- Disinfectant wipes or cleaner and towels for spot cleaning the box and surrounding area
- Clean litter for refilling box
- You may also have a litter mat outside the box that catches litter when your cat leaves the box

The key to successful litter box maintenance is to create a routine. First, make a habit of cleaning the litter box at the same time every day. Maybe it's first thing in the morning when you get up, or right as you get home from work. Find a time that makes sense to you and stick with it.

You're best served setting up your environment to make it really easy to complete your routine every time. Grab a clean bag, put it in the trash bin, grab the scooper (that's always in the same place!), scoop, grab the disinfecting wipes for a quick clean, sweep up any loose litter, take the trash bag outside for disposal. Done!

If everything is organized in one place, you won't be running all over the house looking for a trash bag, trying to find the scoop, locating the wipes. These are the kinds of barriers that make people avoid scooping the litter box. Try to make it easy on yourself; even if you're not generally an organized person in other areas of your life, try it here. It will make your life easier and your cat happier when she always has a clean litter box.

Litter Chest Keeps Things Organized

Lisa Roth, San Francisco, California

© Lisa Roth

Lisa designed this custom litter chest to conceal her cats' litter box and keep all the litter supplies close at hand. The roomy storage chest measures 27 inches deep by 44 inches long by 25 inches tall, leaving her cats plenty of room inside.

The chest has a slat top, attached with a piano hinge, which allows air to circulate and light to enter. Lisa lined the bottom of the chest with a rubber mat to keep litter from tracking outside, plus she can take the mat out and hose it down when it needs a good cleaning.

Inside the chest, Lisa uses a large storage bin for the actual litter box, since she has some elevator-butt cats. Plastic bags and the litter scoop hang on a hook, and the small trash can for scooping fits inside, too. The dustpan and brush are stashed next to the trash bucket. The entire chest opens up for easy cleaning, a feature Lisa insisted on.

Lisa says that if she had more room, she would have made the chest a little longer so she could store the clean litter inside, too. Our only suggestion would be to add a second opening to prevent ambushes, but otherwise, this is a great design!

© Lisa Roth

Easy Litter Catcher

Perforated decking tiles make great litter catchers! These plastic tiles snap together to create any size area for underneath and around your litter box. The loose litter will fall through the openings in the tile, reducing the amount that is tracked around your house. Simply vacuum under the tiles as needed to pick up litter, and when the tiles need extra cleaning, just wash them off in the sink or with a hose. These kinds of tiles are available from flooring supply stores or online, and they come in a wide variety of colors.

© Kate Benjamin

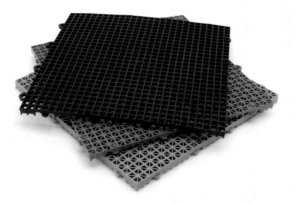

KEEPING KIDS AND DOGS OUT OF THE LITTER BOX

Many cat households have to deal with another big issue: keeping dogs and/or kids out of the litter box. For a kid, the litter box looks like a fun sandbox to play in, and for dogs, well, it's like a snack bar. Both things we're pretty sure you want to avoid.

Many cat guardians find top-entry litter boxes or other litter box enclosures helpful when it comes to keeping dogs and kids out of the litter box.

Baby gates, like this one from Wenchi Liu of Ontario, California, are another possibility for cordoning off the litter box area. You'll need to look for a gate that is low enough for your

cat to jump over but high enough to keep others out.

Try this! Wedge the baby gate into place with enough room for cats to go under, but not dogs or kids. Giving the cats a choice to go over or under minimizes the chance that they will avoid the area.

TOP: Submitted by Shannon Heath, San Antonio, Texas.

BOTTOM RIGHT: Submitted by Nicole from Glen Rock, Pennsylvania.

© Wenchi Liu

Baby Gate Catification Hack

Submitted by Cathy Diaz, Newbury Park, California

Cathy needed to figure out how to keep her dogs out of the litter box but still allow the cats to have easy access. Since her dogs could jump any gate that the cats could jump, Cathy had to install a taller gate with a small door at the bottom. Unfortunately, the door was big enough for the dogs to fit through, but Cathy got creative and pulled a true MacGyver with this hack! In the middle of the door opening she suspended an embroidery hoop that only the cats can fit through. Problem solved! And pretty creatively, too!

© Cathy Diaz

CONSIDERATIONS FOR CONCEALING THE LITTER BOX

Now, if you're really never going to put the litter box out in the open (and even the litter screen won't do the trick), and you absolutely, positively want to hide it, we have some guidelines that we'd like you to follow.

Keep in mind the following when purchasing or building a litter box enclosure:

- Can your cat stand up tall without bumping the top of the enclosure with his ears or tail?
- Can he turn around comfortably inside the enclosure?

- Is the opening large enough for him to comfortably enter and exit?
- Are there multiple openings to prevent an ambush?
- Is there enough air circulation inside and around the enclosure?
- How easy is it to open the enclosure for scooping and regular cleaning?
- Is the inside of the enclosure sealed so liquids and litter won't get trapped in cracks?

All of these considerations affect how your cat and you both interact with the litter box, and any one of them could cause an upset. Creating a litter box enclosure is something that requires you to do your homework in order to get it right.

Try It Before You Catify It!

Why not test out your idea for a litter box enclosure first by getting a large cardboard box that's the size of the enclosure you're thinking about? Cut the openings where you're planning to put them and place the cardboard box with your cat's litter box inside in the spot where you want to put the enclosure. This is a cheap and easy way to see what your cat thinks. You can refine the design with your cardboard prototype before you build or buy.

On the following pages we've gathered some examples from Catification Nation showing creative ways to disguise the litter box. We hope these projects serve as inspiration as you tackle this tricky issue.

Repurposed Cabinet with Cute Kitty Cutouts

Submitted by Chris and Michelle Tan, Orlando, Florida

Michelle and her husband Chris created this attractive litter area for their cats by repurposing an old dresser they found on Craigslist. They cut two adorable cat-shaped openings in the doors and added high-sided plastic boxes inside the cabinet. The cabinet also became the base of their bathroom sink, putting the litter boxes in a great location since the humans use this bathroom regularly. The two openings are perfect for preventing ambushes, but remember: this counts as only one litter box!

© Chris & Michelle Tan

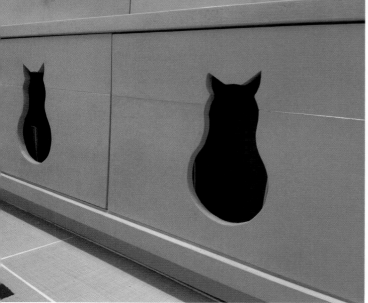

Architectural Inspiration for Concealing the Litter Box

Submitted by Kelly Kacmar,
Valencia, California

Kelly's husband happens to be an architect, so he put his training to the test when he designed this beautiful litter box concealer. What's great about it is that it's large and roomy and lets in lots of light. There are cat doors on both ends and the whole backside is open. Simply roll the whole thing away from the wall to access the box for scooping. The litter pan sits inside a larger wooden tray with low sides to catch loose litter, and there's even a place to hang the scoop. And guess where the litter box is? In the dining room! We approve!

© Kelly Kacmar

Patrick's Cat End Table

Submitted by Patrick Debnar, Eaton Rapids, Michigan

Patrick wanted to create a litter box enclosure to disguise the litter box in his central living space. Now, keep in mind: Patrick has some serious woodworking skills, so we don't expect you to do exactly what he's done. He did include some fabulous details that we want to highlight, which you can incorporate into your own DIY litter cabinet.

First, there are two entrances, one on each side, so no one can get trapped, and look at what Patrick did with the litter box. It's recessed into the bottom of the cabinet

so cats walk in through the door and simply step into the box. This would be great for senior cats or cats with mobility issues. There's also a cutaway carpet surrounding the box to catch loose litter.

The doors are attached with European hinges that allow them to open all the way out for easy cleaning. The oak finish makes the cabinet fit seamlessly into the overall décor, disguising the litter box completely.

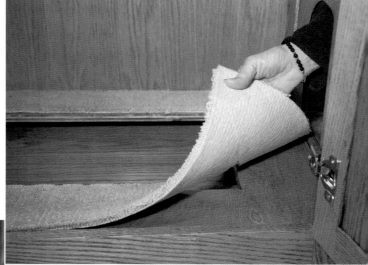

© Sandra Debnar

Wood Crate Litter Hider

Submitted by Britta Becker,
Vancouver, British Columbia, Canada

Sometimes repurposed items make the best litter enclosures. That's definitely the case with this lovely enclosure that Britta made with some old wood crates she had sitting around her woodworking shop. She cut an opening in one side and added doors that swing open. For easy cleaning, she also caulked the seams and lined the interior with acrylic. Of course, we'd like to see a second opening, but otherwise this is quite an attractive solution.

© Britta Becker

CREATIVE REPURPOSING

Here are some other creatively repurposed hacks from Catification Nation. Most need a second opening, but that can be easily added. Be inspired!

Antique chicken coop
Emily McRaney, Biloxi, Mississippi

Storage chest
Jen Rost, San Francisco, California

Trunk
Julia Kirby, Portland, Maine

Kitchen bench

K. Michelle Burgess, Chicago, Illinois

Nightstand
Dawn Clements, Houston, Texas

Be Proactive!

Maybe you say you don't have any litter box issues and you have only one litter box and three cats, or you've hidden the litter box away in the basement. Well, that might be true for now, but things could change. Lots of situations could cause an imbalance. When it comes to litter box problems, you want to be proactive, not reactive. The last thing you want to do is course-correct after things go wrong; it's better if you get ahead on this one!

faces in the nation

Greg Krueger,
St. James, Minnesota

Greg Krueger has mastered the art of thinking like a cat and has used the insights he's gained over the past fifteen years to create a spectacular feline-friendly home for his beloved "fur kids."

G reg's cats are his family, so of course he wants to make them comfortable and provide them with the richest life possible. Luckily, Catification comes naturally to him.

Greg's approach to Catification is unique. You see, he has been diagnosed with Asperger's syndrome (AS), a disorder on the autism spectrum that causes him to focus intensely on details—something that you could say has fueled his Catification projects, along with his love for cats.

Asperger's syndrome is also characterized by an inability to pick up on social cues. As a result, people with AS have a difficult time connecting with others and are often perceived as aloof. Since cats are often perceived in the same way, it comes as no surprise that Greg developed a special bond with his cats. As we explore Greg's home, it'll become clear that behind his obvious skills and dedication to his craft stands a world where two species can meet effortlessly at the communicative fence that used to define them, relaxing in the knowledge that they are finally understood.

"I love cats so much because they are such great, affectionate companions," Greg says.

© *Jeff Newton*

"They seem to possess a sixth sense, intuitive above and beyond our five senses. When I am feeling down and out, sick or just plain out of sorts, they seem to sense that and rally by my side, providing me with love and comfort. Without any words from me, they seem to know everything I am feeling and thinking. Anyone who loves and cares for a cat is rewarded immensely."

> I have always loved being around cats—they are what makes this house feel like a home.

Over the years, Greg has slowly created a kitty paradise by handcrafting walkways, passages, perches and other elements to give his cats places to explore and call their own. From the beginning, Greg has always asked himself, "What would the cats build if they could do it themselves?" By putting himself in their place, Greg has designed one successful project after another.

© Jeff Newton

To create his cat paradise, Greg has assembled an extensive woodworking shop in his garage, as well as another work area in his basement. Greg adds tools as he needs them for each project and has developed his skills as he goes.

Some of Greg's projects may appear to require advanced woodworking skills, but he says that's not the most important thing when it comes to Catification. "I'd like to tell people who say that they have no woodworking skills or that they are not good at making things that I actually got a D- in woodworking class in high school. In my mind, my home does not reflect great woodworking skills; it reflects a lot of love for my cats."

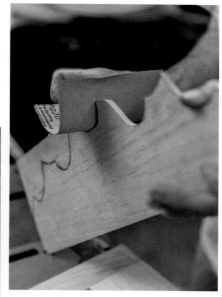

Bubble window looking into Greg's garage shop so the cats can watch him work. They aren't allowed in for safety reasons!

GREG'S CATIO

One of the first Catification projects Greg tackled was building an outdoor enclosure for his cats. He wanted to create a space where the cats could experience the outside but still be safe. The enclosure measures 10 feet by 10 feet by 6 feet tall and is connected to the house with a walkway and two cat flaps. Greg filled the "catio" with plants, carefully selecting varieties that are safe for cats. He says that his cats love the oat grass the best.

A catio is, of course, a great way to give your cats safe access to the outdoors, but if it's not an option, Greg recommends having lots of places inside where cats can look out the windows and enjoy Cat TV (see page 204 for more on Cat TV)!

© Jeff Newton

ENDLESS SUPERHIGHWAY

When you visit Greg's home, probably the most noticeable feature is the elaborate cat super-highway that extends throughout the whole house. Greg has installed about a football field's length of walkways, with thirty-eight openings and a dozen cat stairways.

Greg observed that his cats like to be up high, so he knew he had to accommodate them. He started adding walkways, one area at a time. As soon as each section was finished, he noticed the cats looking beyond the end of the path, so he

kept going, adding more walkways and openings. Greg just kept connecting to the places where the cats were looking to go.

Tunnels and bridges are helpful in connecting the walkways. Greg loves trails and paths, so his superhighway projects combine this passion with his passion for cats. Greg points out that cats can leap from one area to another, but when they are close to the ceiling they cannot always get enough of an arc when they jump, so bridges and tunnels help make the path safe.

Don't Forget the Destinations!

In addition to walkways and steps, Greg has added larger platforms as destinations along the superhighway. These platforms make great places to nap!

With such extensive walkways you might wonder if the cats ever get lost, but Greg assures us that they do just fine. "Cats learn the superhighway routes so well they know the quickest way from one place in the house to another," he tells us.

One important safety tip that Greg adheres to is to always make sure you can see and access every place that your cats can go, including all parts of your superhighway.

STAIRWAYS

Cat stairways provide on- and off-ramps for Greg's superhighway; plus the cats love using them as perches and lookouts. "My cats love stairways. Sometimes they go up part way and stop. Sometimes they go up and come right back down."

Greg's first stairway project was a spiral staircase in the entry to his home. This stairway has fifty steps, each made from 2×4s measuring about 9 inches long. Greg simply drilled holes in each step, threaded all the steps onto a ½-inch steel rod, and then attached each step to the step below with a screw. The result is a beautiful spiral stairway that his cats love.

© Jeff Newton

SAFETY FIRST!

As you can imagine, there's usually a lot of running and playing on the walkways at Greg's house, so he needed to make sure all areas were safe. He added railings to any part of the super-highway where a cat might potentially feel uncomfortable. The railings are primarily for safety, but they also add a decorative element.

"Cats are agile and have excellent balance," Greg reminds us, "but mine have no interest in performing risky gymnastic stunts (unless perhaps there is food involved). So I installed railings on some of the high beams that the cats wouldn't use, and now they not only cross those high beams without fear, but they sometimes actually sleep on them, too."

© Jeff Newton

WALL OPENINGS

Other distinctive features found throughout Greg's house are the many wall openings that allow cats to pass through from one room to the next. Wall openings really make a great superhighway since cats can navigate from room to room without touching the ground. Sometimes Greg's cats just hang out on the walkways and watch through the openings to see what's going on in the next room.

Greg uses three different types of wall openings in his home:

Shaped: These wall openings have unique shapes that make interesting decorative elements. Some of the shaped openings in Greg's house include cat and bird silhouettes, hearts, geometric shapes and even Charlie Brown!

Some of Greg's shaped wall openings.

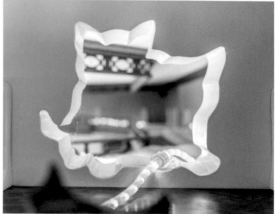

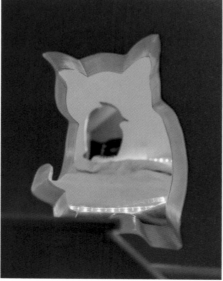

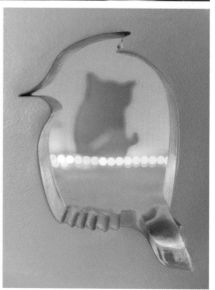

Framed: Sometimes Greg creates decorative wood frames with molding to simply trim the wall openings, adding to the architectural quality.

Cat Flap: Certain areas that are connected to an outdoor catio may require adding a cat flap door to the wall opening in order to protect against weather, hot or cold temperatures, or insects. Cat flap openings can also be blocked off with a board or built-in door.

A framed wall opening.

A wall opening with a cat flap door that is blocked off.

Greg's Tips—Installing Wall Openings

Here are some tips from Greg for creating wall openings as part of your superhighway:

- You may need to adjust the location of the opening depending on what's inside the wall (studs, wiring, etc.).
- The height of the opening may be determined by the height of the walkway if it's near the ceiling.
- For shaped openings, try to make the bottom surface as flat and level as possible so cats will be comfortable stepping across the opening.
- Use wood filler instead of plastic wood, plaster or vinyl spackling, which can all crack and be difficult to sand.

Greg planning to make a shaped wall opening.

© Jeff Newton

LOW-INTERFERENCE CATIFICATION. Greg adheres to the concept of "Low-Interference Catification." In other words, his goal is to seamlessly integrate his Catification projects into his home without making them obtrusive. "I don't want the Catification in my home to look overwhelming. I try to make things so they complement and add beauty to the room," Greg says. "I don't want to bump into, walk around or have difficulty moving a structure when cleaning."

IT'S NEVER DONE

Greg says that having Asperger's syndrome can sometimes prevent him from seeing the big picture since he is so focused on the details. This may work to his advantage when it comes to Catification since he tackles one project at a time rather than being overwhelmed by trying to do too much at once. This is a great example to learn from, since you want to keep in mind that Catification is never done—you can always add on or make changes as your cats change over time. Don't be overwhelmed by how much you think should be done; just start with a small project and go from there.

"I like watching my fur kids using the things that I've made for them. Just by watching and studying my cats, it is easy to come up with ideas. Cats are good at stimulating one's imagination. I love to design and make things. I am currently working on a cat project in my garage. I love the entire process and do not care about when it will be finished. While I do not always know what my fur kids will like most about a project until it is finished, I always know they will not complain about my effort.

"I want to share a bit of advice to anyone who is making something for your cats. Do not worry about making mistakes. Sometimes when I make mistakes I have to think of creative ways to correct them. This often makes a project more interesting than I originally thought."

4

cat superhighways:
navigating the vertical world

In *Catification* we introduced the concept of the cat superhighway. This is a path that allows a cat to access the vertical world and, ideally, navigate all the way around a room without touching the ground. Here we're going to take a closer look at what makes a good cat superhighway by showing you some great examples from the members of Catification Nation.

Cat Superhighways

When I first started using the term "cat superhighway" many years ago, I thought it was a simple way to explain the complicated relationship a cat has with the vertical world. It's become a bit of a linguistic double-edged sword: on one hand, it's catchy enough to stick in one's mind and become, as I had hoped, an integral way of seeing the world as cats do; on the other hand, many see it as a "cute term." So why is that so bad? Because "cute," in my head, can be easily dismissed, and watered down to mean "trivial." The cat superhighway is anything but trivial—it is an essential component of the greater picture that is Cat Mojo.

Giving cats access to every point on the vertical axis in major social areas of their territory is not a luxury, or at least it shouldn't be. Let's go back to the basics of Cat Mojo.

In order for animals that are both prey and predator to feel safe and confident, they *must* feel like they have multiple escape routes from threats and they *must* be able to hunt from a vantage point that gives them as much scope as possible from an angle unattainable by their prey.

The superhighway is particularly essential in homes with multiple animals and/or children. If you doubt this at all, just observe your cats' behavior during the most socially active times of your day (usually when you first wake up, then when everyone gathers after work/school around dinnertime). If you have children and/or dogs, most likely at least one of your cats will spend time looking to get away from the chaotic foot traffic—and that means looking toward the heavens. For many cats, finding peace means separation from other beings; and it just so happens that the other species that occupy their territory live firmly on the ground. The cat superhighway is the one surefire way to provide something that every cat needs: *vertical sanity*.

© Maggie Swanson, PAWS (Pet Animal Welfare Society), Norwalk, Connecticut

YOUR CAT SUPERHIGHWAY TOOL KIT

A good superhighway is all about efficient traffic flow. As with a real highway, there are some key features that help keep things moving along and make the superhighway engaging for your cats. These features include: multiple lanes and levels, on/off-ramps, rest stops, destinations, traffic circles, diffusion posts and hubs. As you plan your superhighway, you'll want to consider all of these elements.

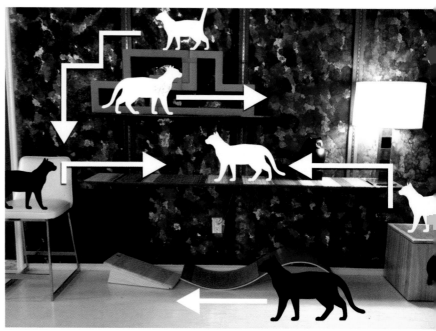

Your cat superhighway can have many levels.

© Kate Benjamin

Multiple Lanes and Levels

In a multicat household, it's essential to include multiple lanes along your superhighway. This is the only way to avoid traffic jams! When you think about traffic lanes for your cats, consider all the levels. A superhighway doesn't have to be just up near the ceiling. Make use of the floor, furniture and low shelves. All it takes is a little strategic positioning and thinking like a cat.

Buffy, Spike and Sofie, submitted by Demetro and Jennifer Karvetski, Warsaw, Virginia.

Wide Lanes Are Better!

People often ask us "How wide do cat shelves need to be?" We recommend eight to nine inches minimum for the width so a cat can walk comfortably, but when you have multiple cats using the same lanes, wider is better. Ideally, two cats should have enough room to pass each other when traveling in opposite directions on the same pathway. Twelve inches will usually be sufficient. If that's not possible, make sure there's an alternate lane nearby so one cat can choose another path.

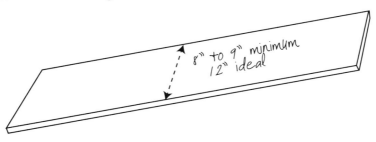

8" to 9" minimum
12" ideal

JACKSON TALKS ABOUT . . .

Just Because They Can Doesn't Mean They Will

I think there's a tendency we all have when setting up cat superhighways that inevitably leads to frustration on the parts of both the cats and the humans. When deciding where a connecting piece goes (to link shelf to shelf, or furniture to shelf, for example), we tend to give our cats a bit too much credit when it comes to their amazing physical abilities. Look at the picture on page 145.

Even positive reinforcement techniques like trailing a toy or placing treats where the two shelves connect wouldn't work here—the cats were choosing to abandon their superhighway, opting instead to go from the floor to the bed to the shelves above the bed. Much head-scratching ensued. Was it the surface of the shelves? Or was the shelf insecurely fastened to the wall?

Sometimes it's not enough just to put on your cat glasses; every now and again, you need to ask the question "What would *I* do?" For example, think about when you're planning your living room layout. If you have a small table where you put your TV remote, you're probably going to put it within reach of where you sit. Why would you put it over . . . *there*? You imagine yourself having to get up and retrieve the remote every time you want to change the channel, and opt instead for the path of least resistance and most convenience. When your living room is done, everything will be at arm's reach, from your drink to your popcorn to your remote.

Is this laziness on our part? If that's what you want to call it, then so be it. And it's okay for our cats to be just as lazy as we can be. So think about why you're constructing something and whom you're constructing it for. If it's an agility course you're going for, then by all means create

Submitted by Mark Galbraith and Catalina Gonzalez, Los Angeles, California.

jumps that challenge and gaps that test their very cat-ness. If it's a superhighway you're going for—if the goal is to create both a transit route and a place of rest that is just as comfortable and traversable as the floor—remember that just because your cat can jump that far, it doesn't mean he will.

Types of Dwellers

Cats dwell in "the confident where"—in other words, that place on the vertical axis they habituate in order to express their cat mojo. Below, we identify three general types of dwellers to help you understand where your cat is the most confident.

BEACH DWELLERS are confident on the floor with all paws firmly on the ground. This is their territory. You tend to trip over them since they will often "own" the center of the room. It's as if they are saying to anyone who wants to get to the other side of the room, "This is mine. If you want it, walk around me."

TREE DWELLERS feel confidence and safety up somewhere off the ground, be it on a chair, a table or the top of the couch. Tree Dwellers should not be confused with Wallflowers—in reality, they are the opposite. The Tree Dweller never hides, but rather displays Mojo by finding a high spot in the vertical world to survey their domain, not to hide from possible predators.

BUSH DWELLERS like to lurk in the shadows. They are natural ground-based hunters who are most confident in spots that are down low and hidden from view. From this spot they are able to survey territory, stalk prey and rest with ease.

On-Ramps and Off-Ramps

On- and off-ramps are simply entry and exit points along the superhighway, but they don't have to be literal ramps. They can be a series of steps, a well-placed tiered cat tree, or any other platform that can serve as a launching or landing pad, with one goal in mind: to eliminate unnecessary challenges that may dissuade your cats from using the superhighway.

It's more challenging for some cats than others to jump up to get on the highway—those that aren't tree dwellers by nature have a harder time. That's what makes on- and off-ramps absolutely crucial. Will your cats use their ramps every time they enter and exit? Most likely not, especially as they gain confidence. But options keep things fresh, interesting and inviting.

BENEFITS

THERE ARE SEVERAL KEY BENEFITS TO PROVIDING ON- AND OFF-RAMPS:

They encourage your cats to use their verticality by providing them with easy and safe access points for entry to and exit from the superhighway. This is especially important for bush dwellers when they first discover the ramps and begin to explore them.

In our experience, cats need on their superhighway what any finely tuned sports car needs: a highway with smooth transitions that will allow them to maintain their momentum.

Ramps are especially useful for both older cats and those with physical challenges. Like wheelchair ramps, they allow entry (or exit) into an otherwise inaccessible area, easing these cats upward and respecting their limitations.

© Kate Benjamin

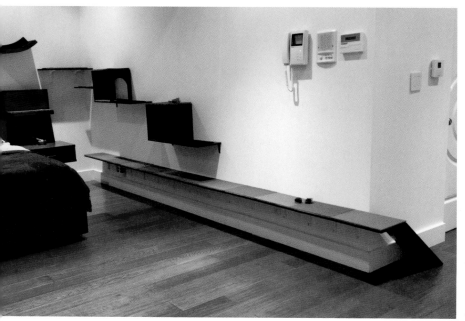

Here's an example of a ramp used to ease the cats up onto the superhighway. This ramp leads from the entrance to the room and wraps around the corner to the lowest lane of traffic.

Wraparound ramp from Mark Galbraith and Catalina Gonzalez, Los Angeles, California.

Kali loves her ramp!
Submitted by Melinda Evans
from Newport News, Virginia.

Ramps and Other Superhighway Training Wheels

It's asking a lot of a cat, especially one who has always known a floor-level existence, to begin vertical exploration. On-ramps and off-ramps become, in this case, superhighway training wheels, opening up the brave new world in a more gentle way. The training wheels, paired with play and reward, can help introduce a new level of Cat Mojo (literally!) and vertical freedom to your companion.

Use your cat's favorite wand toy, trailing it across the floor. Allow him to catch it a few times and start the chase again, just as you would normally play. Start by doing it near the ramp, eventually trailing it up the ramp. Go just as far as he is comfortable, then ZIP, right back down. Back up, just a little farther, and ZIP! Use his natural hunt momentum to get him to forget about his challenge line being crossed.

Place a reward at the top of the ramp, where he can see it as he's climbing. Then, when he reaches his destination, present the reward and lead him back down again, getting him used to the idea that he can enter and exit at will. Start spacing the reward further and further down the superhighway, leading him to the beginning every time he hits his challenge line. Eventually the challenge will be extinguished, and then the real fun begins!

Training wheels can be used when constructing a vertically based agility course or just a tricky intersection of superhighway. If a particular jump just seems scary, place a small piece of temporary shelving between points A and B so the jump can be broken down into two semichallenging steps instead of one super scary jump. Use the play/reward technique, and then, when ready, remove the training wheels.

REST STOPS AND DESTINATIONS

There's a saying that encapsulates rule number one: "It's not the destination but the journey that matters most." When we go on road trips, we pick the most picturesque locations as our rest stops. For cats, that equates to the highest area, the most central vantage point to survey the entire room, and, hey, a cushy rest stop is a good one as well.

A rest stop needs very little besides a shelf and perhaps a soft bed held in place with double-sided tape or Velcro. A destination, however, encourages hunkering down rather than transience. Cocoon-type elements and placement away from traffic can accomplish this goal.

Cat Archetypes

- **The Mojito Cat** is the first of three cat archetypes. She is a social, outgoing cat, confident in her ownership of territory. This cat is practically oozing Cat Mojo, so much so that she will come to strangers, rubbing up against them, even following them from room to room and encouraging these newcomers to pet her. If she were human, she'd be the ultimate hostess, greeting you at the door with a tray of mojitos—"Welcome! Come on in! We're so excited to have you!"
- **The Wallflower Cat** is the second cat archetype. The Wallflower is a cat who displays his lack of Cat Mojo (or territorial confidence), by slinking around the periphery, avoiding confrontation at all costs, deferring, and often becoming overly fearful and shy. The Wallflower tends to be the victim in multicat homes, a role often referred to as "the pariah." In such homes, you would find him caving in the closet or under the bed, or sometimes cornering himself on a shelf or on top of the fridge.
- **The Napoleon Cat** is the third cat archetype, also known as "The Over-Owner." The Napoleon is a cat who displays his lack of Mojo by showing that he owns what he ultimately fears that he doesn't. Such displays include: spraying, aggressive posturing and bullying. Similar to the original Napoleon, and true to the complex that is his namesake, he is paranoid about the prospects of takeover and overcompensates accordingly.

Different destinations serve different types of cats. A Mojito Cat wants, as always, to be the center of attention. A Wallflower's destination should be in close proximity to an exit like a door (or a cat door) and should be removed a bit further from traffic lanes. In road trip terms, think of this as the "scenic overlook" (for a great example of this, see Kate's bedroom on page 162). Corner placement is good for those who feel vulnerable because enveloping walls are like cocoons and provide a sense of invisibility from the madding crowd (Danielle Southcott nails this one in her "Ultimate Cat Den" on page 172).

Remember, however, that destinations can (and in our opinion, should) contain elements of challenge. As guardians, we have an obligation to balance comfort and challenge. You can actually build a destination that is *too comfortable*, where a wallflower can feel invisible and winds up pretty much living there. You definitely don't want superhighway destinations to foster caving behavior. Just make sure that rest stops, which are more open and available to the rest of the world, contain the elements that destinations have, so that your scaredy-cats will cross their challenge lines with a measure of ease. In other words, it shouldn't be all or nothing in the world of ubercomfort. Everything in moderation!

Think of it this way: rest stops are smaller shelves where a cat can stop along the path, while destinations are larger areas with some kind of a reward, like a soft bed or a sunny window.

Traffic Circles, Diffusion Posts and Hubs

Now that we've laid the foundation for our superhighway—building lanes, exits, ramps and the other foundational pieces—it's time to address another crucial transportation principle: traffic flow. It's a certainty that whoever built the first human superhighway realized that speed isn't everything; stop signs, traffic lights and other devices prevent automotive anarchy—and that applies to cats as well.

Traffic circles are generally recognized in the world of urban planning as the safest way to funnel many vehicles into a central location and deposit them at a controlled speed to multiple destinations without the need for intersections (and without the inevitable head-on collisions that can happen in intersections). As you no doubt have noticed by now, Catification is in many ways urban planning for cats, and traffic circles are just as integral a principle in our

Maximus, Jasmine and Rajah demonstrate proper use of rest stops and destinations along their superhighway. Submitted by Amy and David Dudley from Garner, North Carolina.

world. Add a traffic circle anywhere in your home where you may have had conflict between cats. This can be on or off the floor!

Diffusion posts offer an alternate route and are similar to traffic circles in that they diffuse potential conflict arising from head-on traffic.

Diffusion Posts

I remember very clearly the home I was working in when I came up with the idea of the diffusion post. We were dealing with five cats in a very small home. My client worked from home, and over time, her office became the most socially significant spot in the house. All five cats would gather there and compete for the prime real estate, which included a large window, a cat tree and my client's desk.

Our biggest problem cat was a textbook Napoleon Cat and Beach Dweller named Sara. She would camp out in the middle of the room, daring the others to walk past her. If you walked in the door of the office, she'd be tracking your movements. Try to go to the window? Uh-uh. You were slapped down. The desk? Same result. Nobody went anywhere without paying Sara.

We had installed a beautiful superhighway throughout the house, but the office still remained a sticking point. As I stood at the doorway, arms folded, watching Sara swallow the entire transport system like a sinkhole, I asked myself the simple question, "What if we just turned the sinkhole inside out?" What I wanted was to make the center of the room both a traffic circle and a multicat destination at the same time.

It was as simple as putting a five-foot cat tree smack in the middle of the room. My client wasn't exactly thrilled at first, but was willing to make the square footage concession in the name of peace. It worked perfectly. Our beach dweller at first tried to pull her bullying shenanigans but quickly realized that with the blockade in place, everyone else could just choose an alternate route around her. Eventually, she chose to abandon the beach in favor of a tree-dwelling life; she picked the lowest cubbyhole on the tree, and felt confident watching the proceedings. It gave her a feeling of control without *having to control*.

As for the others, they found much mojo in their abilities to get around our now ex-bully, and they'd come to terms with the idea of sharing the space enough to at least call a ceasefire. The diffusion post was born. Conflicts are avoided by using the principle of the traffic circle. Head-on collisions were a thing of the past. And all five cats settled into the system of time-sharing common in more harmonious multicat homes. Not only was there a newfound sense of security and confidence among Wallflowers and Napoleons alike, but the post also acted as an ancillary on-ramp to the highway because the room was so small.

I've used the diffusion post, as well as the urban planning concept of traffic circles, ever since, and it has rarely failed me.

This cat tower serves as both a diffusion post and a traffic circle in Kate's living room. When two cats are coming toward each other from different parts of the room—on a collision course in the middle of the floor—the tower serves as a diffusion post because one cat jumps up onto the tower while the second cat keeps going. It also creates a traffic circle when both cats circle around the tower on opposite sides. Positioning a cat tower in a room right where conflicts have happened can really help diffuse the situation. The key is to allow plenty of room on all four sides of the tower so there are no dead ends.

© Kate Benjamin

Hubs take the traffic-circle organizing principle and simply bring it to the vertical world. They diffuse and steer the flow of traffic. It's important to remember that, whether on the wall or on the floor, good traffic circles don't just reduce fights between cats; they create an opportunity for harmony. Looking at the diagrams below, you can imagine how two cats who have trouble sharing the same chunk of floor-based real estate can coexist harmoniously in a place where they occupy equally important but different vantage points in the vertical world. Another vital advantage to hub building is the idea of variety, of keeping the space fresh and for some, in a subtle way, pushing their challenge line.

.

🐾 hub design

The following shelf configurations can be used to create hubs along your cat superhighway.

BUILD FOR THE CHALLENGE LINE

When planning your superhighway, you want to design for your cat's challenge line. It's important to build for comfort and challenge at the same time. That's how you build for the life cycle of your cat: take the long view. Just as you would help cavers become comfortable leaving the closet, you should encourage them to traverse the vertical world. Every component of Catification should balance comfort and challenge. This will help your cats explore the superhighway. It will also build mojo and help them explore life with confidence and courage.

It's like building a bookshelf for your child. Of course you'll include children's books, but you'll also want to include the encyclopedia set, too.

We want our kids to be curious and to explore, to decide whether they want to be a doctor or an artist. The world of cat parenting, in many ways, is no different. Building your superhighway with their challenge line in mind is very simply building for their potential.

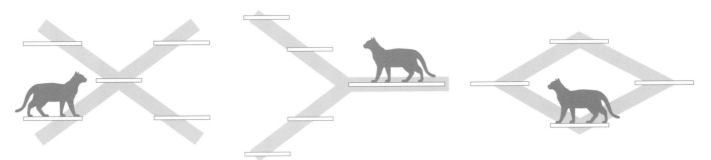

CONSTANTLY EVOLVING DESIGN

We want to encourage you to create a skeleton that can be expanded over time with the climbing abilities of your cat. Let's say there's a hub in the middle of a wall and you have shelves leading up to it. It allows you to create new routes, as your cat gets older. Think about adding ramps and lower shelves.

Hubs remind us to always keep one eye on the scalability of our superhighway. How can we expand and change the pathway? Hubs give you an opportunity to make the skeleton more adaptable to different configurations. The road less travelled will be the road without a rest stop or destination. You never know how your cat superhighway will evolve over the lifetime of your cat. We leave it up to them to cross their challenge line.

Kate's Pro Tip

The Ideal Distance Between Shelves

When hanging shelves vertically, try to space them at about your cat's eye level. This will allow your cat to clearly see what's happening on the next level so she'll know that the coast is clear before jumping up; plus, it will leave enough room between the shelves for her to navigate underneath the top shelf comfortably.

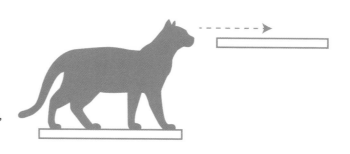

Jenny's Super-Duper Superhighway

Submitted by Jenny Clements,
Logan, Utah

Jenny has created an excellent superhighway packed with features that her cats love. In her living room, she has added two long shelves over the large picture windows and a wraparound shelf leading over to the dining area. The cats have three on/off-ramps: step shelves by the dining room window leading to the upper walkway, access from the top of a cabinet and a wall perch between the two large windows, and another entrance/exit via a baker's rack and step shelf at the opposite end of the superhighway.

© Jenny Clements

The baker's rack allows Jenny's cat to climb up the graduated shelves to access the superhighway. Jenny made sure to add sturdy nonslip surfaces to each level.

The wall perch in between the windows is an excellent hack! Jenny took a curved scratcher that's normally used on the floor and attached it to the wall with L-brackets, creating an inviting perch. Her cat jumps from the sofa to the top of the cabinet and then up to the perch.

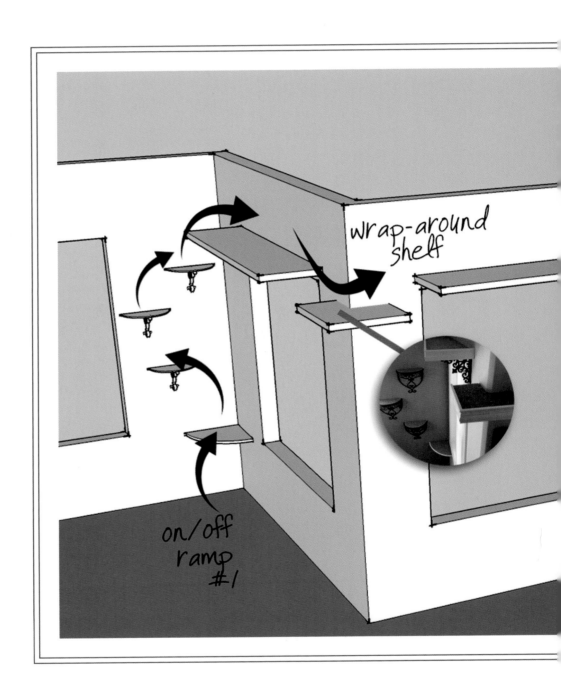

wrap-around
shelf

on/off
ramp
#1

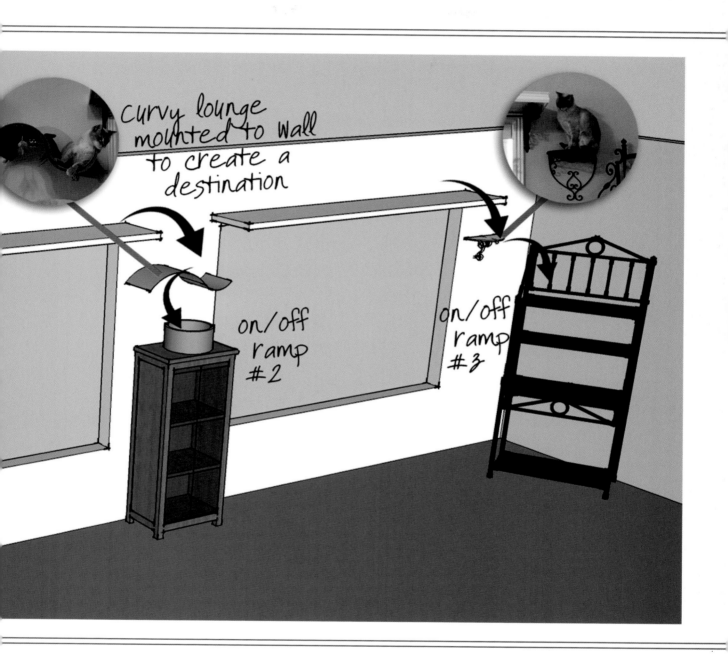

curvy lounge mounted to Wall to create a destination

on/off ramp #2

on/off ramp #3

Jenny added decorative molding to the edges of her cat shelves, which gives them a more formal look and also adds a ledge to keep her cat from falling off. She painted the trim white and added carpet on top, held in place with upholstery tacks.

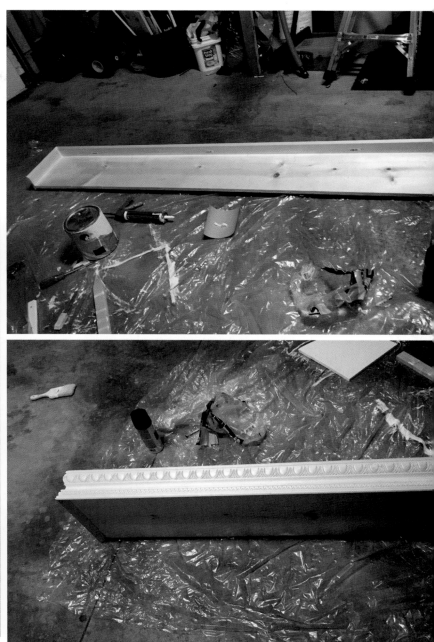

© Jenny Clements

Kate's Hidden Stairway to Kitty Heaven

Here's a project I recently tackled in my own bedroom. I installed the cat tree on the left a while ago, but since it didn't go anywhere, it didn't get much use. I knew I needed to extend the superhighway out from the top of the tree and add destinations and an alternate on/off-ramp. I added the large white wardrobe units, creating a nice, deep surface where cats can hang out, then put up a shelf to connect from the top of the tree, across the doorway opening, to the wardrobe. This floating shelf lets the cats peer down on either side, which they love! I added a yoga mat (makes a great nonslip surface!) to the top of the wardrobes and a comfy cat bed—the perfect scenic overlook destination!

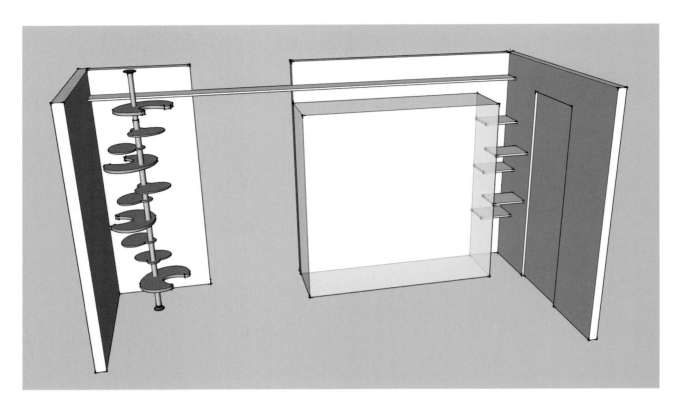

There was a gap about 14 inches wide on the right side of the wardrobes, so I built a hidden staircase, giving the cats an alternate way to get up and down. The steps hang between the wall and the side of the wardrobe and are covered with carpet tiles to prevent slipping. Everyone loves their new climbing wall, and I love watching them use it.

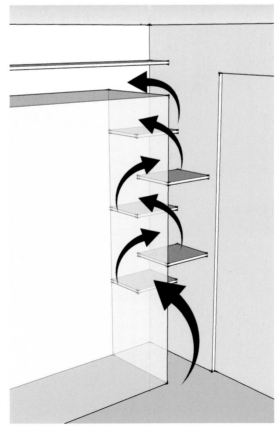

© Kate Benjamin

Yoga Mats Again!

We mentioned yoga mats as alternative scratching surfaces in chapter 2. Well, they also make great cat shelf liners. The nonslip surface is perfect for adding some traction to slippery cat shelves, plus they're really easy to cut to any size. And again, if you use your old yoga mat, it will have your scent on it already, adding to the attraction of the destination.

© Kate Benjamin

Moss Entertainment Center Climbing Wall

*Submitted by Rosemary and Todd Moss,
Tempe, Arizona*

Rosemary and Todd decided to convert their
built-in entertainment center into a cat climbing
paradise. They had their handyman simply cut
openings through the shelves and finish them
off with drywall, and there you have it—a seamlessly integrated cat climber!

© Rosemary and Todd Moss

I actually helped Rosemary and Todd with this design, and we encountered some interesting things during the process. When we first came up with the idea to punch through the entertainment center shelves, I noticed that the distance between the two shelves was quite deep, probably deeper than a cat would want to jump through to get to the level above. I proposed adding step shelves to make it easier for cautious kitties to venture up and down through the openings.

Rosemary then did a little "Try it before you catify it" in order to figure out the final design of the step shelves. She experimented by placing an upside-down basket under the new shelf opening. She learned a couple of things: (1) the cats did like to use the step shelf to get up through the opening, but they were fine jumping down without using the step shelf, and (2) Maya, their dominant black kitty, tended to sit on the step shelf and block the opening so other cats couldn't get through. As a result of her research and experimentation, Rosemary decided to add a step shelf on just one side, and she made the shelf small so Maya wouldn't have room to stop there and guard the opening.

—*Kate*

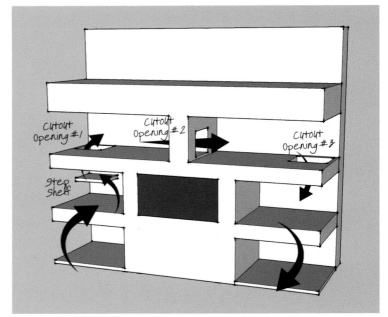

Cutting and finishing the opening in
the entertainment center wall

Maya guarding the opening on the temporary step shelf.

The final step shelf added to one side of the entertainment center is small enough to discourage cats from lounging on the step and guarding the opening.

Maya climbing down through shelf opening without step shelf.

The Ultimate Cat Den

Submitted by Danielle and John Southcott,
Whitchurch, Shropshire, United Kingdom

Danielle and her husband completely catified their spare bedroom, creating the ultimate cat den. They added climbing shelves and fabulous corner perch boxes up near the ceiling. The room makes a perfect base camp for when visitors arrive and the cats need a place to get away. It also demonstrates the concept of building with the cats' challenge line in mind. As the cats become more comfortable with the presence of others, they will choose to come down from their corner hideaway and perhaps sit on the shelves that trail lower and lower, until they wind up on the floor—a brave place to be for a cat afraid of strangers!

© Danielle and John Southcott

cat superhighways: navigating the vertical world   *175*

Custom Cat Climbing Boxes

Submitted by Diane Arendt, Portland, Oregon

© Diane Arendt

When Diane moved into a small condo, she had these custom boxes built to match the architecture and to give her cats extra vertical space to spread out.

© Amy Plankis

I was a die-hard dog person for years and years, in spite of having a great cat when I was little. For some reason I got it in my head that dogs were better than cats, and I remained resolute for over fifteen years. Then one fateful evening, I drove by a cat lying in the middle of the street near my house. I stopped my car to see if it had a collar, or at the very least to shoo it from the street. I had no desire to see a squished cat in the morning. Long story short, the cat tricked me and found a new home in the process. My home. I named him Tyson Li. The cat was such a badass to me that I had to name him after the boxing badass Mike Tyson and the martial arts badass Jet Li. Unfortunately Tyson had a heartbreaking accident and left me devastated beyond what I could have ever imagined. One thing I knew for sure—I had to have another cat. And what's better than one cat?? Two cats. So now I have two wonderful boys, Gideon and Walter. I still have my dogs, but am so in love with my cats that I can't even begin to tell you. The cats say, "Jump," and I gladly reply, "How high?"

This was a very inexpensive project. I had this decorative shelf in my living room but had no desire to fill it because decorations would require so much dusting. So it sat empty for years. The shelves and brackets are from IKEA. The cats were kittens when I originally put the shelves up, but now they are full-grown cats. I think I will be rearranging the shelves in the near future so it will be easier for them to maneuver.

—AMY PLANKIS, CONROE, TEXAS

Dash's Window Destination

Submitted by Paulinka De Rochemont, Rhode Island

When Dash showed up at Paulinka's house as an eight-week-old kitten, she wasn't sure if he would integrate well with her three big dogs; but Dash was fully integrated into the family in no time. In order to give him a little more space to get up and away from the dogs, Paulinka created these lovely climbing shelves that give Dash access to a sunny window over the door—the perfect destination! Now everyone has plenty of space.

© *Paulinka de Rochemont*

I wanted to create a more interesting space for my cat since she's very active and curious; she's also always cold. We have really high ceilings, so adding shelving up the wall to the top of a cabinet has made her quite happy. It's warmer and she has a better view of all the birds outside.

—JACKIE BINGHAM, NEW YORK, NEW YORK

© Jackie Bingham

Dora, submitted by Tom and Linda Pelo, Parker, Colorado.

We have three indoor cats and I wanted to provide them more play space as well as access to higher spaces and windows. What is the point of those architectural Aztec ledges anyway except to collect dust?!

Now they can go up "steps" from the cat tree to get to the shelves, make a left turn and go up on top of the bookcases to see out the smaller window and continue on up the Aztec ledges over the TV for a nap or continue on down the other side to more bookcases and another window. They can also make a right turn from the bookcases and go onto the high shelf to see out of the upper window 24/7 since there are no blinds covering it, and the bird feeders and squirrels are out that way. They all love the new Catification!

—GINA DEGRAZIA RESSNER, LOUISVILLE, COLORADO

Catification Hack: Ikea Lack Cat Climber

Submitted by Sue Mounsey, Bristol, England

Sue was inspired by the Catification Hack in our first book, and she expanded the idea even further. Sue tackled the IKEA LACK shelf hack, a project using two LACK shelves to create a cat climber, this time using three shelves and creating some double-wide platforms. She also added a kitty staircase, creating an alternate on/off-ramp. Great job, Sue!

© Sue Mounsey

Koti and I recently moved into an apartment after living with my parents and their three cats. I was nervous about how Koti would react to living without all the activity of our last home. I was lucky enough to move into an apartment with tall ceilings and very wide window moldings. . . . It was just a matter of filling in the gaps with shelves!

I ordered antique iron brackets to enhance the style of the apartment and put Velcro and carpet on each shelf. I chose neutral colors to match my style and enlisted the help of my handy dad to do the heavy lifting (or should I say drilling).

Koti loves flying up the vertical post and watching the turtle (Cat TV) from above!

She definitely prefers to scratch on her superhighway, and there are multiple textures and styles for her to choose from (vertical, horizontal, carpet, sisal, etc.). She loves sitting by the window to watch the birds and listen to her favorite music while I'm out!

—JEN C., ROCKLAND COUNTY, NEW YORK

© Jen C.

A Colorful Superhighway in Brooklyn

Submitted by Irene R. Boniece, Brooklyn, New York

Irene's superhighway is packed with awesome features for her six cats. Not only can they navigate all the way around a room without touching the floor, but they can also move easily from room to room through the wall openings. She has created all kinds of comfortable rest stops and destinations; for example, she extended the cat shelves out in front of the windows to provide her cats with a view outside.

"I have six rescued cats," Irene says. "Five of them are okay with each other, but Homer is a bully and likes to stalk Ruby and Henry, who both act like prey. Ruby was living in my walk-in closet. I made an extra shelf for her and put in several cat beds, a litter pan and a feeding area. But it was sad that she wouldn't come out. So to provide her with a safe route out of the closet I created a cat door leading to the superhighway. I made sure there are multiple methods of egress along the superhighway and she is now out and about with the other cats!"

© Irene R. Boniece

© Irene R. Boniece

Artwork by Jeremy Gilbert-Rolfe
and Domenico Paulon

cat superhighways: navigating the vertical world

I live in a one-bedroom apartment with my adopted cat, Penny. She is a great, loving, Mojito Cat who loves attention from people. But she also likes to scratch carpet. Now, renting an apartment means that if the carpet is ruined, I don't get my security deposit back, so I came up with the idea to provide her with not only an appropriate scratching surface, but also a place to climb, since a one-bedroom apartment is fairly small. I took an old, wooden ladder and converted it into a cat tree with various carpeted and sisal rope surfaces. She loves her ladder and runs up to greet me by the door every day. Best of all—no more scratching the living room carpet!

Penny lost use of one of her eyes when she was a very young kitten born to a feral mother. She and her littermates were taken to a no-kill shelter in the area, and when I went in, she was the only one left of her litter who hadn't been adopted, presumably because of her eye. But I just fell in love with her, and I adopted her at four months old. I treated her infected eye for a few months, but now Penny is a beautiful, fun-loving cat whose one-eye handicap doesn't stop her from anything!

—EMILY BENNER, PITTSBURGH, PENNSYLVANIA

Catification Hack:
Bookshelf Climber

Submitted by Ekaterina Patrova, Russia

Ekaterina took a regular old bookshelf and converted it into a cat climbing play station. A soft pad makes a cozy perch under a warm lamp, and kitty's carrier is stored on the bottom shelf with the door removed so it can be used as a cocoon. There's a cushion on the very top that can be accessed from nearby climbing shelves, and some cat grass grows suspended below the top shelf.

© Ekaterina Petrova/play-cat.ru

NATURAL CAT TREES

Catification doesn't have to be expensive! Fallen tree limbs can make great cat trees. Here are a couple of examples from the members of Catification Nation.

Submitted by Pablo Druetta, Houston, Texas

© Pablo Druetta

We read *Catification*," Pablo says, "and even though we already had several cat trees around the house, the book gave us ideas to help our cats love their environment even more. We have three cats with different personalities and we really wanted to bring the mojo and confidence out in them. Two of them would fight several times a day because of the lack of a superhighway. There was one main road into the kitchen and living area where the cats like to hang out most of the time, and whenever they were in the same space, hissing and swatting would occur. We felt that we needed to create alternative paths and different seating areas so we could reduce their fighting. Since installing the superhighway and cat tree, we have seen a significant reduction of fights, and the cats seem to be more relaxed and at peace with their new environment."

© Pablo Druetta

Pablo wanted to add nonslip surfaces to the steps so he purchased felt sheets with an adhesive back at the craft supply store. Simply cut to the right size, peel off the paper backing and stick. Great idea! He also purchased faux leaf branches, which he attached to the tree with zip ties.

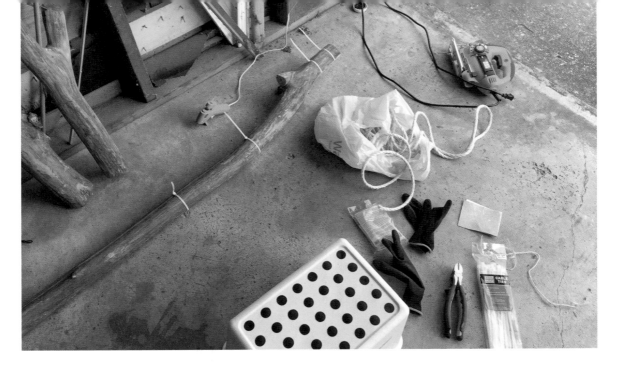

He found the base for the tree in the IKEA scratch and dent section—a great place to find random pieces of furniture that can easily become Catification hacks! The shelves are made from scrap wood, and Pablo bought the sisal rope to wrap around the tree, and screws and L-brackets to secure the tree to the base and to the wall. He spent about $23 on this project.

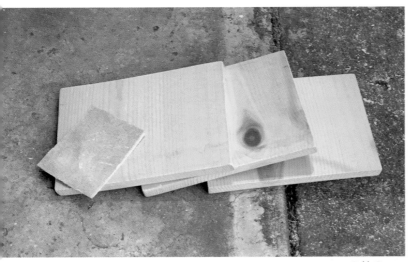

© Pablo Druetta

*Submitted by Jessica Johnson
and Nick Lanzaretta, Mentor, Ohio*

Jessica and Nick used a fallen tree trunk to create this great climbing tree for their cats Vinny and Karl. The tree leads to a long shelf above and includes sisal rope for scratching at the bottom. Another great example of Catification creativity!

© Jessica Johnson

You create **CAT TV** by setting up a special area in your home where your cat can enjoy visual stimulation, ideally watching their natural prey. This can be looking out a window at a bird feeder or other wildlife, watching fish and other critters in an aquarium or terrarium, or even watching an actual television with videos of wildlife.

Wallaby, Lee Jackson and Sparty enjoying Cat TV.
Submitted by Kacy Turner from Fairfax, Virginia.

CAT TV

When planning the destinations along your cat superhighway, don't forget to add some Cat TV! Make sure your cat has a comfy place inside, right by the window, to watch what's going on outside. Try adding a bird feeder outside or a garden with flowers that attract interesting birds and insects.

Remember, cats don't sleep nearly as much as we think they do when we are away during the day. They actually spend the majority of their time, if the space is available, looking out the window. For our little hunters, this is a great way to keep them entertained. You can provide a measure of what Jackson calls "passive engagement," keeping those hunting skills sharp even while resting. This will help ensure that when the energy level of your home spikes in the evening, your cat won't match that energy in a destructive way (of course, make sure there are plenty of toys available inside the home as well to siphon off the energy that remains).

In our experience, Cat TV is an invaluable and vital Catification element. All you have to do is notice the difference in your cats when you come home—they are more naturally centered and grounded because they've spent the whole day doing something AND just standing there!

Candy Cane loves her birdfeeder Cat TV.
Submitted by Dunja Hein, Goffstown, New Hampshire.

© David Weyman

We really like to use cat trees in our house since we can position them in front of a window to create Cat TV. In one case we put a cat tree where two windows come together in a corner. This provides our cats with unlimited visual activity all day. We put a hummingbird feeder just outside the window, and during the spring, they chatter at the hummingbirds.

—DAVID WEYMAN, WIMBERLEY, TEXAS

We turned our new six-foot garden window into a kitty entertainment center. There are several lilac trees in front of this window and hummingbird feeders in the trees, plus we leave seed on the ground for the quail and rabbits. Lots of activity to keep our guys entertained. There are also beds on the top shelf for warm naps on a sunny day.

—LAURIE LAMB, COUPEVILLE, WASHINGTON

© Laurie Lamb

CLOCKWISE FROM TOP LEFT:

Cheetah, submitted by Catherine MacPherson from Stoney Creek, Ontario, Canada.

Smeagol and Roo, submitted by Christina R. from Scottdale, Georgia.

Kitchi, submitted by David Weyman fro Wimberley, Texas.

Felix, submitted by Dallas Marshall from Omaha, Nebraska.

CLOCKWISE FROM TOP LEFT:

TJ, submitted by Eileen B. Brown from Hedgesville, West Virginia.

Nessie, submitted by Emelie Blomquist from Lund, Skåne, Sweden.

Harley and Nemo, submitted by Gretchen S. from Acworth, Georgia.

Jebediah Muffin and Saber, submitted by Elmira Utz from Tacoma, Washington.

CLOCKWISE FROM TOP LEFT:

Candy, submitted by Kathryn Richert from southern California.

Hurley, submitted by Jennette and Robin Schuhmann from Virginia Beach, Virginia.

Tigger Chewbacca and Samwise Montgomery, submitted by Patrick and Kate Pacacha from Williamsport, Pennsylvania.

Harley Quinn, submitted by Krystle and Corey Brenman from Robbinsville, New Jersey.

ABOVE: Loki, submitted by Kyndall Scribner from Texarkana, Texas.

LEFT: Jane, Ellie and Kira, submitted by Kylee Benaszeski from Wausau, Wisconsin.

ABOVE: Griffin and Russell, submitted by Lara Mansell from Tupelo, Mississippi.

BELOW: Eli and Mr. Puff, submitted by Laurie Lane from Binghamton, New York.

CLOCKWISE FROM
TOP LEFT:

Loki, submitted by Alex and
Leanne from Hilliard, Ohio.

Binky, submitted by Linda
Rettstatt from Southaven,
Mississippi.

Tato and Callaway,
submitted by Lisa S. from
Whittier, California.

Helios, submitted by
Michelle Rushing from
Panama City, Florida.

Abby, submitted by
Toni Nicholson from
Decatur, Alabama.

Boo, submitted by Susan Facchini from Rutherford, New Jersey.

RIGHT: Blitzen and Ebony, submitted by Katie Knapp from New Tripoli, Pennsylvania.

BELOW: Lily and Mia, submitted by Michelle Kay from Berwick, Victoria, Australia.

faces in the nation

Humane Society of Boulder Valley
Boulder, Colorado.

© Jeff Newton

catify to satisfy: shelter style

This is the story of how Boulder Humane—Jackson's original training ground—brought Catification to shelter design in order to satisfy the shelter workers and visitors, and of course the cats.

Almost exactly twenty years ago—when I was a musician in search of a day job to sustain me financially—I came across a want ad for an entry-level "Animal Welfare Associate" position at the Humane Society of Boulder Valley (HSBV). My immediate reaction was a shrug of the shoulders, as I thought, "Why not do something to help animals and pay the rent at the same time?" Landing that job wound up sustaining me in ways I never would have imagined. My passion was ignited, and the flame has not died down since. It's a pretty remarkable (and sometimes unsettling) feeling to be able to say, "This spot, right here—this is where everything changed."

Bridgette Chesne was hired just a few months after me in the same entry-level position, and we quickly became not just coworkers but part of a family and "compadres" in the cause. We both worked a number of different jobs in the shelter, serving the whole but looking for our own place in it at the same time. In 2002, Bridgette became the shelter manager. The remarkable thing is not just that she stayed in the position (now called Director of Shelter Services) for thirteen years—an

Courtesy of Humane Society of Boulder Valley

incredible feat in an industry known for burning out its workers—but that she has never once rested on her laurels. Bridgette is always asking why the status quo exists, whether it serves the animals (and her employees), and if not, how she can help change it. Our journeys, both individually and together as shelter workers, helped create the space we are featuring in this profile.

The original building that housed HSBV was a challenge to catify; it was common knowledge that it had outlived its usefulness years before. We were constantly propping up the sagging architecture in a literal sense. Figuratively, we were also finding ourselves unable to keep up with the changing landscape in the industry as it related to housing animals. Newer shelters were embracing the concept that less-stressed animals stayed healthier while in their care and, ultimately, were adopted quicker.

In 1998, after an intensive capital campaign that lasted quite a few years, HSBV's new building opened, directly behind where the old one stood. All of us who had called the shelter our own were excited to see the building go up. But at the same time, there was a sense of mourning: the ragtag spirit contained in that broken building was something owned by our tightly knit crew. We wondered whether we would lose our communal sense of purpose and passion once we moved into the backyard behemoth.

Courtesy of Humane Society of Boulder Valley

Even though I was involved with the design of the cat area, I couldn't help but feel a bit disappointed, for a reason I couldn't quite put my finger on. On one hand, I was beyond elated to be witness to this brave new sheltering world. Being in a building with state-of-the-art ventilation and soundproofing alone was something worth cheering about. Embracing an open-floor plan for adoptions, rather than the commonly held caged model, was *huge*. It was not lost on me for one second that we had learned from the past and were stepping into a future characterized by a growing empathy for the species. The new design seemed to say, "We *get* cats more completely; we know that cages add stress, and territory is everything to them." I felt so good knowing that the idea of what constituted "sheltering" was evolving. Cages represent the notion of basic care, whereas community rooms are symbols of stewardship.

Something about that space, though, something in the details, didn't work. The shapes of the colony rooms and how we chose to set those spaces up limited the number of cats they could hold and undermined how peacefully they could coexist.

In retrospect, perhaps I was frustrated, because at the time, I couldn't verbalize what was taking shape in my head: city planning for the world of cats—superhighways and escape routes, dead ends and traffic circles. These things were at the tip of my tongue back then, but I needed more experience, more time to bring those concepts to life before I could ask the planning committee to alter its vision.

A few years ago, I visited Boulder during my book tour to promote *Cat Daddy*, and took a day at HSBV to work on the "cat situation" with Bridgette. Back in the day, Bridgette was forced to listen to my endless (and often aimless) rants on the subject of the

cat adoption area. She was always keenly aware of my frustrations with the layout, and the time had come to make a change. Boulder is an incredibly generous community when it comes to their homeless animal population, and Bridgette told me the money was there to reimagine that area. We spent the day kicking around ideas, getting very excited about the prospects. At one point, I brought an idea to the development committee that I don't think made anyone happy: I honestly thought that the cat adoption area should be demolished and given to the dogs, so to speak. There was just too much that had to be done to make it work, in my eyes. I thought, well, maybe we should raise funds for a separate building for the cats! You could hear the bottles of antacid being popped open around the room.

Nonetheless, Bridgette engaged me in a marathon conversation about what I would do if I were constrained to the existing space. I let fly—and then, I let go. As I'm wont to do, I spewed ideas, concepts and passions, hoping that someone else was taking notes, because once something's out of my mouth, a good percentage of it is gone with the wind.

In keeping with who Bridgette is, she wasn't just listening; she was taking meticulous

© Jeff Newton

mental notes. And then, unbeknownst to me, she put those notes into action. I literally didn't speak to her about it from that day forward.

I had no idea that the new and improved cat adoption area had even been unveiled, until a mutual friend wrote to me and said, "You know, I bet Bridgette would love to hear that you approve of the new area, especially since a section of it is dedicated to you." Huh? What? I was flabbergasted, in all honesty. I couldn't believe that Bridgette and HSBV behavoir and health manager, Maggie Schaefer, had taken the ball and run with it—to the point that they never consulted with me again, never asked for clarification and, oh, by the way, didn't even tell me when it was done!

Visiting the new HSBV cat adoption area was a very deep, very emotional experience for me. It's also very difficult to put that experience into words. On the surface, the changes were a face-lift. But underneath, they were something much more.

At one point—as Bridgette and I were being photographed, sitting in a room filled with amazing design elements and very happy cats—time stood perfectly still; I was reminded of the beginning of our journey. I'm sure everyone tends to romanticize about the moments that shaped them ethically, professionally and personally; for Bridgette, myself and a handful of others, HSBV had been a golden cocoon where a number of young, animal-centric idealists were forging their place in the bigger picture of animal welfare.

As I put my arm around Bridgette and the shutter snapped, I could imagine our younger selves witnessing this moment—and feeling proud that the geezers still had their heads on right.

"Pretty cool," I said to Bridgette out of the corner of my mouth, as the flash went off.

"Yeah." She smiled. "Pretty cool."

Talk about taking a project and running with it. After Jackson planted the original seeds for the idea of catifying the cat adoption center, Bridgette teamed up with Maggie Schaefer, HSBV's behavior and health manager, and the two really got the project rolling.

The process of redesigning the cat area was truly organic. Bridgette and Maggie met with the contractor to start planning. They trusted their instincts as they decided what would be best for the cats. "Maggie and I are not officially feline experts," Bridgette tells us. "We're feline experts as in we minor in feline behavior. We love felines. We live with felines. We pay attention. You don't necessarily have to have credentials in feline behavior to create a successful design."

As they planned each room—deciding where to put the perches, shelves and cat trees—Bridgette and Maggie made sure to look for any spots where cats could get trapped. If they found

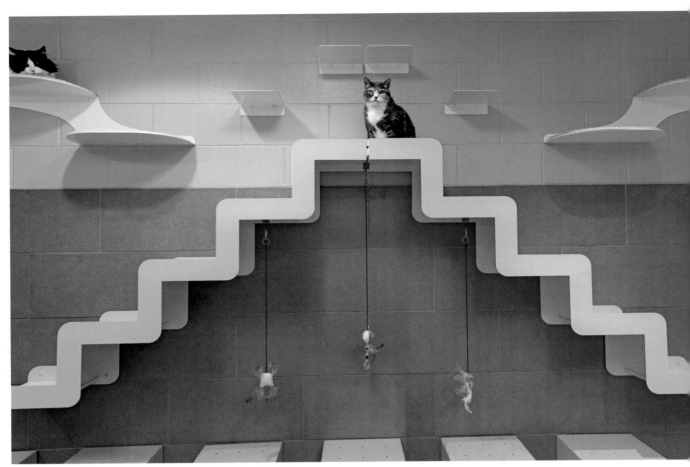

© Jeff Newton

a dead end, they added to the superhighway or made changes to eliminate it. This is so critical in a shelter environment, where multiple cats are sharing the same space, and the population is changing constantly. It's vital to create an environment where cats will immediately feel safe and at ease.

"Maggie and I would stand in some of those rooms for twenty minutes. We were here until 11:00 p.m. most nights during those last eight weeks of the renovation, realizing that we hadn't quite cracked the code," Bridgette remembers. "We asked ourselves, 'What if we did this? What if we did that?' Maggie would say, 'No, because

then I think they're stuck here.' And I'd say, 'Yes, I think you're right.'" These "think like a cat" sessions resulted in spaces that allow cats to navigate freely from the moment they enter a room for the first time, even while they are still adjusting to the space.

Bridgette and Maggie also drew on their experience with their own personal cats as inspiration for the design. "We both have young cats. Maggie has a three-year-old Siamese, Zim, and I have a two-year-old tabby, Oswin," Bridgette tells us. "We were standing in the rooms thinking, 'What would Oswin want? What would Zim want? What would Zim do? What would Oswin do? If Zim and Oswin were both in here, and Oswin was being persistent in bothering Zim, where would Zim go?'

"We just kept bringing our two personal cats back into it because they have very different personalities and, as a result, are a good representation of the cats we see at the shelter. They're both a little bit sensitive and insecure, but they manifest it differently and they interact with other cats differently. So we just imagined what would happen if we forced them to live together here at the shelter. What would they need for that to work?"

The new cat adoption center at HSBV was well-received by humans and felines alike when it was unveiled in the summer of 2014. The space includes lots of creative, functional and beautiful solutions that serve the cats, staff and shelter visitors equally well.

LET THE SUN SHINE IN!

The cage-free cat rooms are bright and colorful, letting in the Colorado sunshine through solar tubes in the roof. The extra sunshine reduces stress levels for the cats and makes the rooms an inviting place for visitors to hang out and spend time playing with or just watching the cats do their thing.

BUILDING THE SUPERHIGHWAY

Bridgette and Maggie were careful to build complete superhighways in each of the separate cat rooms, giving the cats access to the full vertical space and allowing them to navigate all the way around the room. They added multiple lanes at various levels to keep the traffic flowing and to eliminate dead ends. Powder-coated metal shelves and staircases were used throughout, making the walkways easy to sanitize and very durable—both critical features in a shelter environment.

PORTAL? PORTHOLE!

The new design connected two of the smaller rooms with cat doors that could be closed off to divide the rooms or opened to allow cats to move freely back and forth, creating a flexible space. Originally, Bridgette and Maggie discussed cutting mouse holes at the bottom of the wall to connect the rooms, but some creative brainstorming led them to a much better idea.

"We kept saying, 'Portal? What kind of portal?'" Bridgette recalls. "And then Maggie said, 'Porthole.' And that's how it happened. The minute she said 'porthole,' we were on eBay, finding and ordering old ships' portholes. It was just this really fun, creative process. Maggie and I are

© Jeff Newton

compatible that way, and we're both eager and efficient in our thoughts. We were a good team."

Two authentic ship portholes now connect the rooms and can be easily closed off to separate the spaces. The portholes are up higher on the wall, connecting the superhighway on both sides. The addition of colorful fish window decals makes them even more visually interesting and helps the cats to see when the portholes are closed.

NEST BOXES

As you know, we love a good Catification Hack, and the nest boxes at HSBV are a

great example. These metal storage boxes, purchased at an organizing store, are mounted on the walls about ten inches off the ground, creating raised hideaway beds that offer a little privacy. The tops of the boxes also provide additional steps along the cat superhighway.

The boxes are powder-coated metal, like the shelves and stairs, so they are also durable and easy to clean. The cushion design used inside the nest boxes is particularly brilliant for a shelter environment where sanitation is of the utmost importance. The shelter workers place donated towels inside extra large plastic bags and then slide the bags into decorative pillowcases. This makes it easy to remove and wash the pillowcases, replacing the plastic bags only as needed if they become soiled.

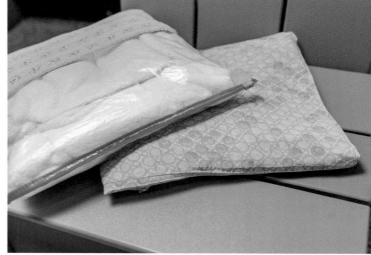

© Jeff Newton

CREATIVE TOY SOLUTIONS

Toys are just as important to a shelter environment as they are to a catified home. Bridgette and Maggie developed some great ideas for keeping the cat toys organized, any of which could easily be used in a home. One idea is to attach decorative bottles and jars to the wall for storing wand toys. This keeps the toys close at hand, but also creates an attractive visual element in the room.

Catification can work on different levels in a shelter than in a home. For shelters, every element of the hanging toy jars *works*. First, they

keep a neat, organized appearance. This affects potential adopters at a subconscious level because they might think having cats would clutter up their home. The jars also serve as a subconscious "call to action" for volunteers and visitors. Strategically located right by the door, the jars invite humans to grab a toy and interact with the cats in a way that is pleasing for both parties. In a way, this actually trains the cats to interact with humans and encourages them to trust and seek attention from people—an important shot of mojo for cats that may have abuse and/or neglect in their past. Not to mention, of course, that nothing will get a cat adopted faster than having a bonding moment with a potential adopter.

© Jeff Newton

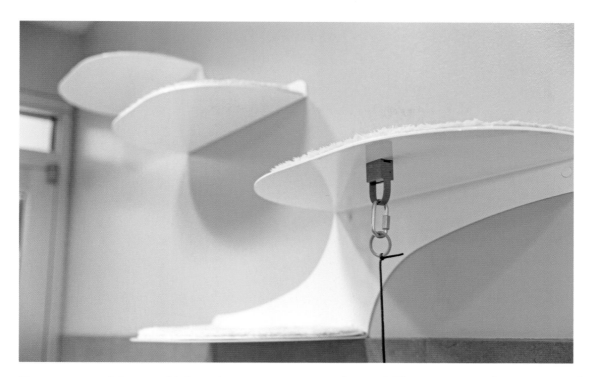

Because most of the superhighway lanes are metal, Bridgette and Maggie got the idea to dangle toys from superstrong magnets underneath the shelves. This is a great way to increase stimulation throughout the room, again adding visual appeal. The magnets can be repositioned so toys are in the places where cats play with them the most, and the toys can be easily replaced when they become worn.

WOODSTOVE CAT BED

In the main cat room, a large utility pipe protrudes from the cement block wall. Instead of simply painting the pipe to match the wall and ignoring it, Bridgette and Maggie decided to paint it black; then they found an old cast-iron woodstove to place in front of the pipe. They propped the doors open and added a comfy cushion inside, and voila! The most popular cat bed in the room! This sturdy structure allows cats to enter through the front or through the opening on the side; plus, cats love to walk across the top and hide out underneath. This hideaway is almost always occupied!

© Jeff Newton

FENDER AMPLIFIER CATIFICATION HACK

And finally, as a tribute to Jackson and his love of music, Bridgette and Maggie created an awesome Catification Hack that the cats just love. It's an old Fender bass combo amp that's been converted into a cat hideaway, for kitties that need a quiet retreat. Holes in both sides of the cabinet (where the handles used to be) allow cats to jump in and out; plus, the front screen is held in place with Velcro and, when removed, reveals the large cutaway originally used for the speaker. This makes it easy to access the inside of the cabinet for cleaning.

This design also gives the staff options when it comes to the specific residents of the room. For instance, if there is one cat who tends to ambush others, the front of the amp can be taken off, allowing the cats to make the choice, day by day, to opt for extraquiet space, or one with an extra exit route to stave off unnecessary tussles. Finally, the amp hack is a perfect example of a furniture piece that caters to both tree-dwelling as well as bush-dwelling cat clients. They can opt for a hideaway or they can survey their domain from the top of the cabinet, which, because of its height and position near the door, serves as the perfect perch.

WORDS OF ADVICE ON SHELTER CATIFICATION

HSBV set aside $100,000 for this renovation, including all structural changes to the building and all purchases to outfit the rooms, but Bridgette wants to tell other shelters not to be discouraged if you don't have that kind of budget to work with. We asked her what advice she'd give to shelter managers who are looking to improve the quality of life for the cats in their care. Where should they start?

"I think that every shelter probably has some kind of small room or closet—an area close to its cat center—that could be assimilated into the cat adoption center, a place that could become a communal living space," she says. "I would say focus on that one area to catify and do some fun things, especially wall-mounted perches and walkways. Add fun toys and interesting things to look at. Make it comfortable for people, too, even if it's small. Find a place where you're comfortable, where cats can lounge and have visitors come and go.

"I think people sometimes have to look at their space and imagine it empty. Not a kennel, not a cat, not a fixture, and kind of say, what *could* it look like?

"We are temporary custodians, and while those animals are here, they should be comfortable. Stress reduction is important. It's all about perception, too. We want people to walk through and say, 'Wow, they take really good care of their animals.'"

Jackson and Bridgette reflect on the new Cat Adoption Center at HSBV:

Jackson: The reason we need to celebrate this room is not just because it's a beautiful, functional room that's really going to make the lives of those cats better—but because it represents how much we've learned in twenty years. And the message is: just do something.

Bridgette: Yes, it really is. It really is as simple as that. Take one small space and just do something.

Jackson: Do anything, but just do something!

conclusion

It seemed as if from the moment the ink dried on *Catification*, your questions came pouring in. While it was a bit overwhelming, to say the least, these questions excited us to no end, since they represented investment on the part of guardians, taking our concepts and approaches to a new level as you took the matter of your cats' happiness into your own hands.

We hope we answered at least most of the pressing questions, and we hope we did so enthusiastically, in big, bold colors. In fact, we hope you noticed that everything we chose to bring to light in these pages was bold—from the approaches to the profiles, from shapes and sizes to locations. In reality, we are just mirroring the gusto with which you have embraced the concept of Catification.

As always, one of our primary objectives is to inspire you to act, *to do something*, to inspire you to make bold choices for your companions' sake. And we hope we succeeded.

Now that we've answered some of your questions, we have a few for you:

Did we get you to catify? To look around your space and consider the possibilities?

We hope the answer is "Yes," of course.

Do you feel like you can better see the world through cat-colored glasses?

Can we get an "AMEN!"?

Do you feel more connected to your cats? Is your relationship stronger? With a little less frustration and a little more love?

Please say "Yes!"

Are your cats satisfied?

If you did anything at all from the pages of this book, we promise you they'd say "Yes!"

And finally . . .

Are you satisfied?

Here (and only here), we hope your answer is a resounding "No." In this particular case, a vote for the negative is a sign of tremendous success. Every moment of inspiration means never being satisfied. Sure, we're allowed our moments of Zen—the singular bliss that comes as you watch your wallflowers bloom, your Napoleon Cats stop to watch the world go by from a place of peace and every cat becomes their own version of Mojito Cat. But then it's back to work—the work of building, expanding and growing, of course, but also, and more important, of empathizing and understanding and connecting the feline dots. The work of bonding with your cat is a journey for sure. And as everyone on this journey can testify, you can stop to admire the view, but then, keep walking.

Walking the walk goes further than your living room and deeper than caring for your animal family. When we encourage you, in a very loud voice, to "catify the world!" it is our sincere hope that at some point, those walls that you have worked so diligently at transforming into a superhighway vanish to reveal something even more super—your extended animal family.

We feel that, as citizens of Catification Nation, we have a duty born of deep love. That duty is to do for the good of the nation, to do for all what we do for some. It's not just *our* cats that are counting on our love, compassion and action—it's *all* cats; and each of us can do *something* for the good of all.

So the next question becomes: if you can't catify the world of every homeless cat, then what steps can you take to make a difference? The answer is actually pretty straightforward:

Adopt, don't shop. Your local shelters and rescue organizations are filled to overflowing and are fighting to save the lives of the homeless; many cats will die while waiting for homes. Let's not stack the deck even higher.

Spay or neuter your cats. Quite simply, there's no reason not to. From health risks down the road to disruptive behaviors in your home do the obvious math: for every kitten that is born, many cats will die for lack of homes. Again, it's the only empathetic, selfless thing to do.

Learn about feral cats. There is a hidden population that numbers in the tens of millions. Band together with your community by calling them *your community's cats*. TNR (Trap-Neuter-Return) has been proven to be the only humane and effective way to control feral populations, and volunteers to do this crucial work are desperately needed.

Volunteer. We've all at one time uttered the phrase "I couldn't go to the shelter—I'd want to take all the cats home with me!" Well, if your house or your life can't accommodate another cat, you can bring your compassion to your local shelters or rescue organizations. You can take the traditional route by signing up to spend some time with the cats—socializing them, fostering, serving as an adoption counselor, or just helping to clean the place! You can also take your Catification know-how to the shelters, helping to build better cat habitats and bettering the lives of cats waiting for their forever homes.

Educate. Spread the word to like-minded humans about the plight of the homeless and inspire them into action.

As we've shown you in this book, just putting up a few shelves constitutes Catification action; as clichéd as it may sound, every little bit helps in the world of your community's cats.

We've been honored to help guide you deeper into your home to uncover the treasures that were waiting for both you and your cats. We want more than anything to continue answering your questions, to witness your discoveries and to help bring them to the rest of the Catification Nation; after all, that's what a true community is all about. Keep checking back at www.catificationnation.com for what comes next. As for the larger world of cats, and making that world better for all of them, go to www.jacksongalaxyfoundation.org to help expand your circle of compassion—and to put your money where your mouth is and your mouth where your heart is. Compassion begins at home; it should never end there.

Until we catify again, here's to you and your cats!

—Jackson and Kate

index

t